LOAN SHARP

Get the business finance you deserve

ROB WARLOW

Loan Sharp - Get The Business Finance You Deserve
© Rob Warlow 2010

Book Cover Design & Typesetting by Zahra Ginieres Ridge

Set in Arial 10 on 15pt

First Edition published in 2010 by;
Ecademy Press Ltd,
48, St Vincent Drive,
St Albans, Herts. AL1 5SJ
Tel: +44 (0)845 003 8848
www.ecademy-press.com
Company Registered in England – 5639586
VAT Registered – 971 4474 02

Printed and Bound by;
Lightning Source in the UK and USA

Printed on acid-free paper from managed forests. This book is printed on demand, so no copies will be remaindered or pulped.

ISBN 978-1-905823-77-2

CONTENTS

ABOUT
THE AUTHOR

After spending 25 years in banking in the UK and Africa Rob now concentrates on helping small and medium sized businesses develop and grow. His main focus is assisting business owners to access finance to start up or grow their businesses.

Too many business owners reduce their chances of getting the finance they need by not understanding what banks are looking for in an 'ideal proposal'. Being a person who has been at the sharp end Rob uses his extensive banking knowledge to help business owners get the right information a bank needs.

In writing Loan Sharp Rob has used his hands on experience to bring the reader practical ideas and solutions to finance their plans and realise their vision.

Rob also writes a weekly newsletter, Small Business Success, distributed via email to 3,000 small business owners which covers a variety of topics of interest to business owners. He lives in Wales with his wife and four children.

Rob can be contacted via **www.businessloanservices.co.uk**

INTRODUCTION

The Bank Manager! The person who has the destiny of your business in his hands! If you are just starting out in business or running an established enterprise, the Bank Manager can be liked, trusted, feared or someone you just plain don't understand. The financial events of recent years have dramatically shifted, and some argue changed forever, the relationship between business owners and banks.

No more cosy days of Captain Mainwaring from Dad's Army; no more the gung-ho and flashy days of the dot-com era; and no more spotted-faced bankers who only knew how to say yes which categorised the mid 2000s!

We are now in a new era where the fresh-faced innocence of bankers and entrepreneurs, who in many cases only knew the good times, is officially at an end. Stories already abound of business owners who have seen banks change their attitude towards their business with little or no warning and in many instances with no perceived logic. When the economy was booming decisions on loans were easy ... it was simply 'yes' ... but now that the boom days are at an end (for a while at least) decisions are equally as easy ... now it's simply 'no'.

With banks making credit extremely difficult to obtain, and during the early days of the recession totally impossible, small businesses have faced challenging conditions not seen in decades. Perversely, despite witnessing the lowest Base Rates for 50 or so years, for many business owners the cost of borrowing has gone up; payment terms by bigger companies are being stretched so putting cash flow under pressure; expansion or start up plans have been put on hold; achieving or maintaining profitability has become a struggle. All of these stresses have meant that more than ever small businesses need the support of banks but in many cases it hasn't been there.

Will Things Change for the Better?

Will this credit drought be with us forever? No. The reactions seen over the last few years are in reality merely knee-jerk; decisions made in haste are overturned in haste and that is what we have seen. We have had bankers running scared and that's mainly because marginal decisions made in good economic conditions often don't stack up when the going gets tough; confidence levels have quickly disappeared and it's easier for banks to say 'no' whilst they concentrate on sorting out their bad debts.

Now here's a 'but' and a big one at that ... the 'good' times you have been used to should not be seen as the norm; it was the credit explosion which was madness, not the credit drought we have recently seen. Essentially, what we are witnessing now will be the norm; we are merely resorting back to how it should be in the first place.

Very soon though banks are going to wake up and realise that they have forgotten one basic principle ... they make money by lending money! They can't stay out of the market forever. Besides, re-entry into the lending market in a significant way will soon be forced upon the older, more traditional players – the competition is coming. The new kids on the block are preparing an assault on the small business market. The new players – the supermarkets, foreign banks and UK-niche financial services providers – are seeing opportunities ready for the taking. There is a big demand for a return to true relationship management and this is one of the gaps to be filled by the new players.

That's why things will change, and change for the better. This is why you need to be prepared.

You Will Also Have to Change

But is it only the banks to blame for the recent mess? No! You are equally to blame. There is joint responsibility for the chaos we have seen. Everybody got used to easy credit, and half baked ideas which should never have seen the light of day were promoted and given the green light. Small business owners got used to not having to fight for credit; a Business Plan? What was that? You now have to understand that the rules of the game have changed and so you have to change as well. You will now have to prove more than ever that you and your business are worthy of support. In tough times, and with memories of recent events to linger for many years, bankers will be strictly following their criteria and lending standards. You have to be prepared for this and the business owners who understand this fact of life are the ones who will be supported once the market truly opens up again.

The purpose of this book is to help you get a better understanding of what banks want from you in readiness for when the banks fling open their doors again. The days of developing a relationship between banker and customer will return. Business owners are crying out for banks to return to the old model where there were Bank Managers on the local patch that had the power to make decisions and the time to understand their clients and their businesses. This is where the new entrants into the banking market are likely to declare the battle ground.

But in preparing for the new order you must remember that a relationship is a two-way street and to expect someone to support you without all the necessary information is the same as asking someone to marry you based on a 30 minute encounter! Sure, it can happen but the chances of getting it wrong are substantially higher. Banking is down to the strength of your relationship – the stronger it is, the greater your chance of success.

I want to give you the edge when it comes to meeting your Bank Manager; I want you to think like him and talk like him; to understand the criteria and standards expected of you. After all, people do business with people they like, the ones they can empathise and connect with, and that comes from speaking the same language and thinking alike. Could you say it has ever been that way for you? Probably not, but it needs to be, going forward.

Banks will still be there to support those companies with a solid track record and an impressive profit history. For them, little will change other than higher lending rates and longer waiting times for an answer. For smaller businesses, where the perceived risk is higher, the challenge will always be there, except for the ones who are prepared to research and train themselves to be a lower risk.

The up-turn will come and yes, things will be different, but by reading this book and following the tips and ideas contained in it you will be better prepared to take advantage and come out the other end smiling and with your finance request granted.

What Will You Learn?

Over the years the methods and the technology may change but the general principles of lending will never change and it's these principles that I'm going to be sharing with you in this book. This is not a textbook full of theory which has little relevancy in real life situations. As a Manager at the sharp end, I've been there; I have seen too many business owners requesting finance who were just not ready or at best ill prepared. They did not present themselves, or their business, in the best light. The result? A resounding 'no'.

Undoubtedly many of them had sound ideas but they were just not convincing enough to get me on their side. How sad. Today, even the best ideas are getting turned away because the immediate reaction of bankers is to say 'no' – as a banker today you can't get into trouble that way! So how can you ever hope to get your business off the ground or expand your already successful business?

The answer is knowledge. Why shouldn't you know what's required of you before you walk through the Bank Manager's door? If it makes life easier for both of you why should it remain a big secret? Well, it doesn't any longer ... the answers are contained within these pages.

Here you will find a blueprint for significantly improving your chances of getting the bank to support you and your business. I will walk you through the banker's thought processes, how to get inside his mind, to show you what he will go for and what he won't.

Here are just some of the things you will learn:

- How to select the right bank

- How to build a relationship with your Manager

- How to read and understand Financial Statements

- The steps to preparing for your interview

- The key questions and issues your Manager will ask and want to know about your business

- How he analyses the information to come to his decision by using a structured framework

- What to do if things start to go wrong

It Doesn't End Here!

Whilst I have tried to include all the possible barriers you will encounter I'm sure some new and unexpected ones will be thrown your way! That's why I have set up a website as a resource base for you. Here you will find more articles and resources to help you on your journey. Simply go to www.businessloanservices.co.uk and see what's going on.

I'm sure that by taking action on what you will learn in this book you will be in a better position to understand what banks are looking for and thereby increase your chances of successfully getting your Bank Manager to say 'yes'.

The last few years have been difficult for people on both sides of the table. With a better understanding of what you can do to even the playing field you'll be approaching the whole ordeal from a much stronger position.

Now here comes the health warning!

Naturally I can't guarantee you will get what you want but with these ideas I know you will be better prepared than if you hadn't read this book.

I look forward to hearing from you with your comments and experiences.

Good luck.

Robert Warlow
Business Loan Services
www.businessloanservices.co.uk
rob@businessloanservices.co.uk

CHOOSING THE RIGHT BANK FOR YOU AND YOUR BUSINESS

Having a good bank and an understanding Bank Manager is one of the key features of a successful and profitable relationship. A good relationship with your banker means that when an opportunity arises or a minor cash flow problem hits you there is someone at the end of a phone to help you through it.

Running a business is never easy and dealing with day-to-day financial challenges means you need a good banking partner behind you.

In this chapter we look at the very start of the client-banker relationship

– the courtship, finding the right partner!

Don't Necessarily Accept What You Have Today

If you are already running an existing business then you probably have a business bank account. You may think that a chapter on searching for a bank account is one you can skip. But should you?

Don't assume that the bank you have now is necessarily the right one for you. A bank can be like a pair of old slippers, they are falling apart, they may not look or smell very pleasant but you have been together for years and the thought of parting company is too much for you to bear, so you stick with them! But Christmas comes, and your kind old mother buys you a new pair. After having reluctantly agreed to part company you suddenly realise you should have thrown the old pair away years ago!

A banking relationship can be like this – you get used to the bank and you tend to overlook the small niggling service issues; besides, it's too much hassle to change isn't it??

No it's not!

You should never let sentimental feelings cloud bad service or persuade you to stay with a bank that doesn't understand you, or can't be bothered to make the effort to understand you.

Now, I know what you are saying ... all banks are the same, why bother changing? In light of recent events, which have witnessed a fundamental shift in the banker/customer relationship, and the horror stories that many small business owners have to share about nearly all banks, you are probably right to wonder if it's worth changing. Is it really more a case of 'better the devil you know'? However, as we saw in the Introduction, the time is coming when competition between banks will return and a clear differentiation will emerge; you need to be ready to take advantage of that change in approach towards small businesses – you will become loved again!

That's why, if you are in business already, you should still read on and think about what you want out of your bank.

How to Choose a Bank

Your success in getting a bank to support your request for finance does depend on you choosing the right bank in the first place. Even if you don't initially intend to borrow any money, keep this possibility in mind when you are researching the market.

With competition increasing you can get some good deals if you are prepared to shop around.

So where should you look and what criteria should you use when searching for a Bank?

Your Existing Bank

If the bank where you hold your personal account offers business banking facilities then this is probably the best place to start. You already know their level of service (good or bad!), the layout of the branch and perhaps even some of the staff if you are lucky! This can make the whole process of opening a new account so much easier.

But don't open your business account at the same bank just because it will be less hassle. You must still ensure that the features of the business account are what you are looking for and of course, that it comes at the right price.

A New Bank

You may decide that service levels in the bank holding your personal account are so poor that you won't waste your time looking at their business account offering! In that case, it's time to pound the streets or boot up your PC to start searching online for the best deal.

Even if you have a good relationship with the bank that has your personal account, don't dismiss the notion of looking around. One reason to consider opening your business account at a different bank is that of total separation between the two aspects of your life – your business and personal life.

Consider whether you want one institution having complete control over your business and personal finances. If you do go through a tough patch in the business, would you feel comfortable with the bank seeing what you have sitting in your personal savings account?

There is great merit in looking to totally divorce your personal and business finances.

Online and Postal Banking

It is possible to have a bank account which is operated online without the need to use a traditional High Street branch. Whilst this can work very well for simple banking needs, for more complex requirements you are better off seeking out a mainstream bank.

If you decide to go down this route satisfy yourself on these points:

- Is there a sign up fee?
- Is there an ongoing monthly or quarterly charge?
- Is the cost per transaction less than a traditional 'bricks and mortar' account?
- Is there an email or message facility in case you have account-related queries and what is the quoted response time?
- Is there a technical support service? If so, is it offered free or will you be charged per minute via your phone cost charge?

However, even if you opt for a traditional account the use of an online facility is extremely useful to keep track of your finances, so seek out a bank which provides this service.

Location

If you have no preference for a particular bank, then the physical location of your branch may be a higher priority, especially if you will be paying in a lot of cash. In this circumstance having a bank just around the corner would be very useful. On the other hand you may feel more comfortable travelling in a car when carrying cash in which case a secure and safe parking facility may be on your wish list.

Some businesses have very simple needs when it comes to banking.

If you don't handle cash or a large volume of cheques and you are happy banking over the telephone or Internet, then location is obviously less of an issue for you. But be mindful that the lack of a 'real person' to talk to could be a frustration when you have a major problem to sort out.

What Products or Services Do You Need and What are You Prepared to Pay?

Prior to your search you need to decide which products or services you will need to help operate your business efficiently. If you are new to the banking game and have no idea about the range of products or services available then start learning! Grab every leaflet and brochure you can find, read all the bank websites and see what products are out there.

Armed with your new-found knowledge it's then time to consider what you are prepared to pay for the privilege of running a business account. Many banks will offer 12 to 18 months' free banking for start ups but if you are a more established business then be prepared for some haggling. If you are seen as a trouble-free account, despite not being a start up, then you still may be able to negotiate a 'no charges' deal if you switch banks.

Trade or Industry Association Deals

If the industry you are in has a large trade association or membership body then you may find they have negotiated a discount or special offer with a particular bank. The discount can come in the form of a limited period of free banking or a permanent reduction on the standard account usage tariff. An example of this is the Federation of Small Businesses which has a free banking member-only deal with the Co-op Bank.

What Relationship Do You Think You Would Have?

I have not mentioned yet probably the most important aspect of banking for many business people – the person who is going to be looking after you; your point of contact to sort out the things that will go wrong! Your Relationship Manager.

If you know that you are going to be borrowing in the near future then ask to see the person you are likely to be dealing with. Like it or not, the success of your loan application is going to be down to the person representing you to the higher authorities.

"My advice to any person is to get a bank that allows a face-to-face relationship. This adds to the building of not only a business relationship but also a potential friendship."
Matt McGrandles, COS Media, www.cos-media.com

Get in front of him or her and ask yourself whether you could get along together. The old adage that 'people do business with people they like' is very true. A good relationship with your banker is important, and is something we will be covering in more depth later on in this book but in summary you are looking for someone:

- Who will provide good service
- Who is a good listener
- Who takes interest in your business
- Who has a grasp for your industry and the issues you may face
- And ideally a Manager who has a personal lending limit (a rare breed!)

The last point is key. Ideally you need to find a bank which understands the need to have someone 'on the ground'. A local Manager, who doesn't have to apply to a Head Office for every single pound to be lent, is the equivalent of finding a gold mine! As I mentioned in the Introduction, niche banks are beginning to understand that this is what small business owners want, so we may yet see a return to the old fashioned Bank Manager. See if you can find one!

Go Hunting

If you have no particular bank in mind, or you are only interested in getting the very best deal, visit or call as many banks as you can so you can make an informed choice. Ask to speak to the Small Business Manager or Small Business Advisor (each bank will have its own job title), tell them you are interested in opening a business account and looking for information.

The good ones will spend time with you, offer you brochures, talk you through the process and the leaflets and tell you about their range of services. How you are treated at this early stage will give you a good idea of how you are likely to be treated later on. If you are met with indifference, or a puzzled look following your queries, then you know it's time to swiftly move on!

Could You Do Business With This Bank?

Once you have done all your research, got feedback from business colleagues and tested the initial reception you received, take some time to assess and evaluate all the information you have gathered. To help in the process prepare a table which will provide an 'at a glance' summary. On one axis list each bank and on the other list what you need from your ideal bank. Then simply put a 'yes' or 'no' to symbolise whether the bank has met or failed to meet your requirements.

Take a look at the sample table on the next page.

	OFFERS ALL THE ACCOUNTS I NEED	COMPETITIVE CHARGES	GOOD SERVICE ON INITIAL ENQUIRY	ONLINE BANKING OPTION
BANK A	Y	Y	Y	N
BANK B	Y	N	Y	Y

Once you have populated your table you should then quickly be able to pin-point the bank which best suits your needs. Based on your findings, which bank stands out head and shoulders above the rest? Which one did you feel most comfortable with? Make an informed decision based on all the information you have gathered and then move on to the next stage which is actually opening your account.

Opening a Bank Account

Having made your decision on which bank to choose, go back or ring up and arrange an appointment to start the account opening process. Seeking out a formal appointment is not only the best way to manage your time (who wants to waste valuable hours sitting around waiting in a queue?) but it also starts off your relationship in a professional manner.

Items You Will Need

In this day and age, as with most tasks, you are going to need a stack of papers to get the process started, so be prepared for a paper chase! You can reduce the stress by preparing as much as you can in advance.

You can start your preparation by checking out if the bank has listed its opening requirements on its website. Some may even include a downloadable version of the Account Opening Application Form which you can complete in advance. This means you won't have to make two journeys, one to pick up the forms and the other to drop them back.

Check if you and each partner or director will have to visit the bank personally to open the account. You may not be permitted to complete the forms in the comfort of your office and then post them back to the bank due to the risk of them not identifying you correctly; the bank will want to eyeball you to ensure you match your passport or other photo ID.

Account opening requirements are not going to differ that much from bank to bank but the two principles to follow when putting your documentation together are that the bank will want you to prove:

- You are who you say you are
- You live where you say you live

All of this is guided by Anti Money Laundering requirements (generally known in banking circles as 'Know Your Customer') which are designed to ensure that criminals can't use bank accounts to launder their ill-gotten gains. Banks have a responsibility to correctly identify individuals so they don't unwittingly be party to criminal activities. This can make the account opening process rather laborious and appear to be a perpetual bureaucratic paper chase but there is no way around it. If you are struggling with any of these items then approach your bank and ask what alternative documentation they would be happy with.

DOCUMENTATION REQUIRED TO OPEN YOUR ACCOUNT

- A completed Business Account Opening Application Form
- To identify you personally as the owner, partner or director of the business, identification such as a Passport or Driving Licence

- To confirm your address and as an owner, partner or director of the business, a minimum of one utility bill, which is less than six months old. Alternatively you can present a bank statement, mortgage statement, insurance certificate or Council Tax bill

- If you are trading via a Limited Company you will need the Memorandum and Articles of Association and Certificate of Incorporation

- A Bank Mandate form (supplied by the Bank and usually included in the Account Opening Application Form) showing a specimen signature and confirming who is to sign for Partnerships and Limited Companies

- Possibly a copy of any stationery or letterhead detailing your business name and official address

- Anything else you can think of which will confirm you are in business and proving your primary trading location

- An outline of your business which can be in the form of a Business Plan

- Some banks may even go as far as to ask for a reference from someone you know

Getting Your Account May Not Be That Easy!

You would think that banks are anxious to do business with anyone but in some cases that is far from the truth. Banks like to know that they are dealing with 'respectable' people, so as well as deciding that you are comfortable with them they will also go through a process to decide if they are comfortable with you!

There are two important factors the bank will consider in allowing you to have a business account: the information about you or your business and your credit record.

You and Your Business

One way to encapsulate everything the bank needs to know about you and your business is to present them with your latest Business Plan. Stripped of any sections which relate to bank borrowing (unless that is your ultimate aim) this is a simple document which summarises your business – an overview of you, your business and your future plans.

Whilst you may think that preparing a Business Plan is a bit over the top when all you want is a bank account, it can help. The bank will know you are serious and have thought about your future plans. It costs the bank money to open an account and so having one on the books which will never operate, hence earning them no fee income, is a costly affair.

If you have never attempted to write a Business Plan there is no need to panic as in the next chapter we will look at some key points to cover.

Credit Searches

One way for banks to get to know you is via a credit search. The banks will ask credit reference agencies what information they have about you on their credit reference file. You may not be aware but most people in the UK will have some information about them stored with these agencies.

The agency will confirm, via a range of internal and external sources, positive data such as your address and your presence on the Electoral Roll for example, and any negative data recorded against you. This can include any County Court Judgements or unpaid debts which will be a red flag to the bank that you could be a troublesome customer.

If you are refused an account because of a negative report, or you would like to know what is held on your credit file before you approach a bank, you can request a credit report from any of the agencies. The cost is £2, although some do provide a free report. You can find out more from one of the three main credit reference agencies:

Equifax - www.equifax.co.uk
Experian - www.experian.co.uk
Call Credit - www.callcredit.co.uk

Prior to applying for a loan it's vital you check your Credit File. Errors can and do happen and as banks will do a credit check as part of the loan vetting process you should make sure all the information is correct and up to date.

If you operate via a Limited Company banks can also do a check against the company to ensure the details you supply are correct.

"If you are concerned about a poor credit score there are actions you can take.

1. If your Credit Report says you are not on the Electoral Roll then get on it immediately. Contact the Electoral Office in your area and ask for the application form and/or ask them to send you a letter confirming that you are on the roll. Armed with this you can then get your file updated.

2. Don't be late with credit/store card payments. Set up a monthly Direct Debit to pay off at least the minimum payment every month. If you are late it will be recorded on your file. While once is acceptable twice is not, and it will affect your Credit Score which could then take months to drop off.

3. The same applies if you are late with loan or mortgage payments. If you think you may be unable to make a repayment on time contact your lender before the due date of your payment. They may allow some leeway which will buy you time and save your reputation.

4. Not having credit cards or a history of credit can be as bad as having too much or paying late. Having credit cards and not using them will also do you a disservice. The best strategy is to have at least one credit card in your own name, use it periodically and always pay at least the minimum each month.

5. Do not apply for credit until you know you have a good credit Score. Every unsuccessful application you make for credit will effectively reduce your score and compound the possibility of being rejected. Repeatedly applying for credit can result in you being considered a poor risk by lenders as it indicates that other lenders may have rejected you."

Helen Clover, ECity Finance, www.ecityfinance.co.uk

Once your account is opened, if your ultimate intention is to borrow money, then start as early as you can in establishing a relationship. A strong relationship with your banker is one of the key building blocks in getting the bank to support you.

If you fail to open an account because of a poor credit record some banks do offer a 'starter' account which contains a limited range of services. Whilst not ideal it will at least get you off the ground. Check with your bank to see if they can help.

How to Start Building a Relationship

One of the main factors in getting the Bank Manager on your side is your relationship with her. People much prefer doing business with someone they trust and know – would you buy a product or service from someone you didn't trust? It's the same with your banker – you have a better chance of getting a 'yes' if she trusts you and knows you.

If you are just starting out in business, and you know that you will be applying for a loan or overdraft in the very near future, then once you have opened your account, ask to see a Relationship Manager or the person who will handle your request. Introduce yourself as a new account holder, tell her a bit about your business and that you will be seeking an appointment in the next few months to discuss the possibility of borrowing money.

Don't be tempted to go into the full 'pitch' about your business and why you need to borrow. You are not ready yet and as you don't get many chances to create the right impression, why spoil it at this early stage?

Your aim in seeking this brief 'hello' meeting is to show the Bank Manager that you exist, and to give her a chance to see what a thoroughly nice and trustworthy person you are! Remember when you were chasing your first boyfriend or girlfriend? Nice and easy does it; don't jump in with your size 10s! You are looking to build a long term, solid relationship which will withstand the ups and downs that will invariably come your way. Once you have that, then come the day you are ready to borrow money, all the ground work will have been done.

If you are already in business and borrowing money then you should know who your Relationship Manager is. But how well do you know him? Could you class your relationship as strong? Are you comfortable enough to call him with the smallest of queries? Do you know his mobile number? If not, then you need to look at how you can develop this important relationship.

Here are some pointers on how you can build a longstanding and mutually beneficial relationship.

Trust

No relationship can be established or nurtured if there is no trust between both parties. Trust is the bedrock of a strong relationship. Trust cannot be built at the very start of a relationship; it can only be built over time by demonstrating that you are true to your words and promises and that you act with integrity. Trust is about the willingness to listen, to try out new ideas and is demonstrated and reflected in your actions.

The best way to start building trust is to invite the Manager to see your business in action. Seeing a business on the ground is the best way to understand how it really works; it will give your Manager an insight into the day to day mechanics of how your business operates. However, there is a caveat to the invitation – only invite the bank to your business premises if it conveys the impression you are looking to create!

We'll take a look at this method of relationship building a little later when we see the factors banks take into account when assessing a request.

Respect

When dealing with your Manager you need to understand that he is not running his own business, he is not in charge of his own destiny. There are rules and regulations which you may not like or understand but ultimately it's not his fault. Respecting the fact that his hands are tied on certain decisions will go a long way to building mutual respect. Assuming you are confident that he has represented you fairly, if you blame him for decisions or outcomes beyond his control then his respect for you will diminish and so will his support.

Banks can do strange things sometimes, and if you are looking to build a relationship with a view to borrowing money or to extending the facilities you already have, then don't go looking for constant arguments. Understand how banks make their money and why they do what they do. This doesn't mean rolling over and accepting every decision. By all means query and challenge as after all challenging and questioning demonstrates the type of business person you are. At the end of the day accept what you can't change; don't keep harping on about it otherwise you will put the relationship at risk.

Respect your Relationship Manager's position, the constraints he faces and treat him the way you would wish to be treated. And of course, ask him to do the same for you so that you build mutual respect.

Communicate

Communication is one of the most important aspects in building a relationship. Good communication is down to what you tell your Manager and how you tell her.

What You Tell

The 'what you tell them' is what is going on within your business. Send her quarterly reports which cover the key things which have happened within the business; include your Management Accounts, mention the good deals you have picked up. No one likes surprises, and a regular flow of information will put the bank at ease, especially if you are already borrowing. If you're not borrowing still send the information so that you constantly reinforce the message about what you and your business stand for.

Aim to meet your Manager at least once a year face-to-face, preferably at your office or business premises. Regular updates will quickly build and strengthen the relationship and develop an ongoing understanding of what your business is all about. Be visible.

If you are committed to regular contact then the communication between you and the bank should also include any bad news you may have. Perhaps not so important if you are not borrowing, but if you do have an overdraft limit an early call about a problem, whether large or small, is better that the bank hearing about it through the business grapevine. Your openness is a clear demonstration of your credibility and integrity.

Even if the problem is not a potential business destroyer a phone call to inform, especially if it could disrupt your cash flow, would be appreciated. The willingness to share both good news and bad news will demonstrate that you can manage your business effectively and dispassionately.

How You Tell

The second element of good communication is the 'how you tell it'. Each person has their own preferred style of communication. Some prefer a phone call, others a written update, while some have a preference for face-to-face meetings. The best option is to ask him which method he would prefer. Either way, always follow up a meeting or phone conversation with a letter or information pack. Relationship Managers change and you don't want all that knowledge you have imparted to disappear with him. Get everything into your file so it is there for posterity.

The 'how' is also made up of your communication style. It's back to respect and trust. Your style needs to be one of openness and not combative … save that for the real battles!

Write a Business Plan

Whether you are just starting out or running a successful business already, there is no better way of getting the bank to understand your business than writing a Business Plan. A well prepared and written Business Plan will tell the bank everything they need to know about your business. Such a document is the ideal way to start a relationship as you have immediately provided the basis for understanding how your business works.

As I mentioned earlier we will be looking at a basic Business Plan outline later in this book.

Now we have got the basics out of the way we will next move on to looking at the alternatives to bank finance. Before committing time to approaching the bank, and all the pain associated with this, you should consider all avenues of less costly and less time consuming funding.

BEFORE YOU GO TOO FAR ... DO YOU REALLY NEED TO BORROW?

No doubt you have bought this book because you need help or ideas on how to approach your bank for an overdraft or loan, or you have been turned down and don't know what to do next. But before we get to the strategies you can use to obtain bank finance let's take a step back and consider whether you actually need to borrow any money. Have you looked at all the options or just defaulted to a bank?

I'm sure some of you have heard rumours that getting bank finance has become a bit tricky! No need for me to take a poll on that question. Yes, it has got tougher and now, more than ever, entrepreneurs need to be determined and creative when it comes to sourcing finance. Don't make the mistake of thinking that banks are the only source of finance; they are not.

"My advice to anyone looking for finance is to seek out all other avenues before going to the bank. The bank's approach to assessing a funding request lacks balance in that risk sharing has largely disappeared to the point where the security and terms are outrageous. If you can avoid using bank finance, do so."
Chris Slay, Skills Provision Ltd, www.skillsprovision.co.uk

Of course, nothing comes for free. Whichever source of finance you are looking for it all comes at a cost, be it a fee, an interest charge, a slice of future profits or a general piece of the action. What the alternative sources may give you is a possible 'yes', swifter decision making and less onerous terms and conditions, particularly in respect of the security you are expected to pledge.

So, before we jump into the main part of the book let's take a short diversion and explore other avenues of funding. Consider each of these options as part of your overall financing structure before assuming that the banks are the only financiers you can approach.

Your Savings

If you have carefully planned your entry into self employment then you should have been saving hard. Your savings can be in the form of cash, unit trusts, shares or even a property which you are prepared to sell. Funding your new business or an expansion via savings is cheaper than any other source of finance and, assuming your business is going to be profitable, the rate of return on your investment will be far better than putting it in a flashy savings product! By committing your savings, because you are taking the whole financial burden, you may deem the risk to be high and so you may not favour this option. However, as an entrepreneur you should be an inherent risk-taker.

There is a flip side though. Funding the business yourself means you have no one else to answer to – no banks, no investors - and this gives you total flexibility and freedom. This is the ideal position to be in and may be the deciding factor to dip into the family's inheritance pot.

Just because you think the pressure is off in terms of other people to answer to you should not get complacent. You should invest just as much time and effort into planning as you would if you were approaching a bank for finance. Take a long hard look at how far your savings will stretch to get your business off the ground. Budget all costs and purchases carefully with all 'what if' scenarios covered. You don't want a cash shortfall just before you get going and then have to start the process of approaching the bank to fill the gap. Have a robust finance plan in place and build in a contingency for the inevitable unexpected costs.

If your planning reveals that your savings are not going to be enough and you are adamant you don't want to take on finance then you will have to be more focused in saving enough cash thereby delaying your starting or expansion date. It's better to do this than face going cap in hand to the bank at the last minute to bridge a funding gap.

Keep Your Job for Longer

If you are just starting out in business then you are going to be in one of two positions:

- You still have your job and so you have time to plan and prepare
- You have been made redundant and the entry into the world of self employment is very sudden

If you are in the lucky position of still being in a job consider how long you can hold out before the entrepreneurial urge gets too strong. If you have done your financial planning correctly you may have identified a funding shortfall. Staying in your job can help plug the gap so ensuring a more secure, smoother start.

Could your start up preparation period or first few operating months be run alongside your day job for a short while? A monthly pay cheque could help fund the business during its early loss-making days so lessening the financial burden. Be careful about any contractual obligations you have with your current employer, especially if you are starting a competing business – the last thing you need is an accusation that you have stolen client or product information.

Keeping your job has two benefits. Firstly, you will still be earning thereby allowing more time to build up a cash reserve to either reduce or totally eliminate bank finance.

Secondly, keeping your job is an opportunity to test market demand before making the leap. Naturally you should have convinced yourself of this before committing your funds but it's a good safety net for the crucial first few months.

There is a major point of caution here to take note of - make sure you can realistically keep both balls in the air at the same time otherwise you will end up doing justice to neither your job or your new business. Keeping your job is a great way of de-risking your new venture but the downside is that over a period of time your business is likely to suffer; it will eventually need your full time attention if you are to unleash its true potential. Be wary of staying in the comfort zone of salaried employment for too long; your ambition is to run a business so make sure you keep that objective in focus.

The support of your family is essential if you are to follow this strategy. They have to accept that what used to be 'family time' in terms of evenings and weekends will have to take a back seat until you decide the time is right to concentrate on the business full time.

Suppliers and Other Creditors

Suppliers and creditors can be a source of finance for both established businesses and start ups but for the latter it will be much more difficult. Here, you are simply asking your suppliers if they could wait to be paid for, say, 3 to 6 months after delivery or invoicing, thereby allowing you time to get the business open and generating cash.

Normally for start ups most suppliers will want cash up front. The failure rates amongst start ups are high; many businesses would not be prepared to take the risk of extending credit terms until you have proven your ability to pay. You may be lucky to get, say, 15 days' credit but this is not going to make much difference in taking pressure off your financing needs.

Established businesses may also face the same reluctance, especially for first time orders. The recent poor economic climate, which led to a high number of business closures, taught suppliers that handing out credit was not without risk. You can now expect a much more rigorous assessment or grilling but certainly not along the lines you will have from the banks!

Having said that, if you have the gift of the gab and a terrific idea that appears to be a sure winner, then you may strike lucky and get the breathing space you need. So why not ask!

Family and Friends

This group can be a useful source of finance particularly when banks are less than keen to support you. In recent times, for business owners turned down by banks, this has been the easiest option to go for. Family and friends' investment can be made in the form of a loan (fixed repayment term) or buying shares (repayment via dividends or share buy-back arrangement at a later date), so there is an element of flexibility for you in terms of type and repayment arrangement.

The upside of this type of funding is that family and friends tend to be more trusting and are unlikely to request security as a bank would. Also the return you are expected to give investors would be lower (in some cases perhaps interest-free) than that charged by banks thereby improving your profitability. Money invested from sources such as this may also improve your chances with the bank. Banks like the idea of sharing risk as it shows there are other investors with a stake and an interest in making your business work.

However, involvement of family and friends can bring its own challenges. Whilst this group are people who know and trust you, don't forget that you will be moving into a very different relationship. A business with family and friend investors which hits a cash flow problem or suffers a major setback can put a considerable strain on the relationship, more so than with a bank which is a faceless institution. It's bad enough getting calls from the bank if you have missed your loan repayment but it's even more stressful when your father or your best friend is the one calling you. Could you cope with this added pressure?

What about taking other people's money? Would you sleep well at night knowing that Aunty Flo could lose a chunk of her nest egg? If the bank loses its investment, well that's kind of OK, but your relative? Think this one through; you don't want to be distracted from the job at hand because your thoughts are dominated by fear of losing other people's money.

Once you have thought through the pros and cons and you have made the decision to go ahead who do you approach? If you have harboured ambitions to run your own business for some time, or been in business for a number of years then many of your family and friends are likely to know about your idea or business already. You should therefore have a list of likely candidates who have pre-selected themselves – Uncle Joe who has openly mocked your idea won't be on the list, whereas Dave next door who can't stop asking questions and coming up with ideas will definitely be on your list.

You may have your list but what family and friends are lacking is a thorough understanding of the intricacies of your business; you cannot expect people close to you to risk their money without having an in-depth appreciation of both the potential upside and downside of the investment you are asking them to make. Once you get to the point where you are ready to start pitching for an investment think about hold an Investor Evening. Prepare a presentation outlining your plans, the business, the market etc. Show the potential investors what their return will be in recognition for supporting you. This is your very own Dragons' Den nightmare!

Invite as many people as you can and promise an interesting and fun evening. Be bold at the very start; tell them exactly why they are in the room, so there are no misunderstandings. You should be up front and tell them that you are looking for either cash to finance the whole project (less your contribution of course), or searching for investment to match the finance you will raise from a bank. After you have done your presentation gather the names of people who may want more information or a one-to-one with you.

Once you have your final shortlist send them a copy of your Business Plan which covers your business in more depth, details what you need the money for and how the investment will be repaid. It's essential you provide this document; potential investors must be fully aware of the risk they are taking; all the perceived upsides and downsides should be covered.

By the end of the whole process you will have a list of people who are prepared to invest and all that remains is to formalise the investment. In order to protect both your interests and that of your investors it is vital that a formal document be drawn up which clearly states the agreed terms and conditions, such as interest rates and repayment dates. Misunderstandings between parties because nothing was put in writing can be damaging for your business. It would be advisable to engage your solicitor in preparing the document and you should insist that the investors see their solicitors prior to signature.

Obtaining finance from people you know is not for the faint hearted. It's best avoided if you have other avenues of funding but if other options are limited and you are convinced your business idea or expansion plan will work then it's worth considering.

Mortgage or Equity Release

This alternative source of finance is for those of you who are home owners and have equity in your house. The amount of equity you have is the difference between the value of your home and your mortgage. You can release cash from your home up to a certain percentage of the valuation of your house and subject to affordability of the monthly repayment.

For self employed people raising cash against your house is not as easy as it once was, with the tightening of mortgage criteria by lenders and house prices stagnating and, in many cases, falling over the last few years. Even employed people with steady salaries can find it tough going. But if you are self employed the availability of these mortgages has declined over the last few years following the downturn and at one point it was practically impossible to find a provider. Over time this will change but the task will be tough so the best route is to go via a mortgage broker who will know which providers are in the market, if any!

If you are still employed and yet to make the leap into self employment, then your best plan is to think ahead and apply for the additional mortgage whilst you still have a full time job. Sneaky, but it can work!

The downside of raising finance this way is that whilst the interest rate is likely to be lower than that charged for a business loan, it's still an additional finance cost to bear. You will have no grace period, which is available with business loans where you are given three to six months before you make a repayment; a mortgage means the following month you will have to find the increased payment. If the income source for the monthly repayment is the business then this puts pressure on to either get your new business producing cash immediately or your expansion to start paying for itself very quickly. Can you guarantee this? You will be faced with a dilemma – who do you pay? Your business creditors or your mortgage company?

Following on from this, another downside is that because the cash is raised and secured against your house it's now at risk if the business cannot generate sufficient cash to cover the payment. This is a very real risk which must be discussed with your partner. If you are married and the house is your family home, such pressure can cause immense strain on your personal and family life, so be very sure you can meet the repayments even during a lean period; calculate your ability to repay based on real 'worst' case scenarios.

The upsides of raising finance this way can be enticing though. Firstly it's certainly a cheaper alternative to a bank overdraft or loan. You can also spread the repayment period over a much longer term than with a business loan. Business loan repayment periods are generally between 5 and 10 years whereas mortgages can be repaid over a period of up to 25 years.

Another plus of raising cash this way is that the amount raised would be considered as matched funding by a bank if you need to top up the cash with further finance. Your contribution may not be in the form of cash which was saved but you have clearly demonstrated your commitment to the business by putting your house on the line.

Lastly the process of arranging a mortgage, whilst lengthy, can be less painful than trying to arrange a business loan. As mentioned earlier, if you are self employed, this could be practically impossible especially if your business is a start up or less than 3 years old.

An additional mortgage on your house does have its drawbacks but it can be a less painful way of raising the capital you need.

Non Traditional Lenders

There are companies, other than the traditional High Street banks, which act as prime lenders. These companies use their own funds for lending so there is no middle man. Terms and conditions would be broadly similar to the High Street lenders but the decision making process is usually less bureaucratic. An Internet search for 'business loans' will help you quickly find these companies.

Community Development Finance Institutions

If you live in a disadvantaged community then obtaining finance can be even more difficult. A very useful web resource is Community Development Finance Institutions - **www.cdfa.org.uk**. The organisation brings together a list of independent institutions which provide loans to both businesses and individuals who have been declined finance by the traditional banks. The focus on disadvantaged communities and business owners from ethnic minorities can be a lifeline for entrepreneurs struggling to get finance for viable business ideas.

Credit Unions

Credit Unions are another source of finance which is growing in popularity. Credit Unions are financial co-operatives which are member-owned and controlled. To join you usually have to live in a particular area, work for a certain employer or be part of a community group which has formal links with the Credit Union.

The Union will typically offer a variety of savings accounts and sometimes current accounts. Interest is paid in the form of annual dividends and amounts saved are guaranteed by the Financial Services Compensation Scheme up to £50,000.

Once you have started saving you are able to borrow from the Union. Terms will vary between Unions but the cost can be up to 1% per month but no more than the legal limit of 2% per month. Most will lend up to 10 years with security and 5 years on an unsecured basis.

You can find out where your nearest Credit Union is located by visiting the Association of British Credit Unions' website - **www.abcul.org**

The Prince's Trust

If you are aged 18 to 30 and have a viable business idea then the Prince's Trust can come to your aid. The Prince's Trust Business Programme focuses on people who are unemployed or working less than 16 hours per week. They provide funding up to £4,000 (£5,000 for partnerships) in addition to extensive training programmes and guides.

Understanding that the first few months can be challenging, the Trust allows its recipients to pay only £20 per month for the first six months and the remainder over a period of three years.

You can obtain more information from the Prince's Trust at **www. princes-trust.org.uk**

Credit Cards

If you don't have savings, can't get support from family or friends, or mortgage, then there are your credit cards! These are often 'lender of the last resort' and during recent times, when traditional funding options have dried up, many business owners have turned to their personal credit card to see them through short-term cash flow difficulties.

If you have previously been employed then it's likely that you have built up a reasonable credit limit over the years. If you are planning to branch out on your own then it may be worth applying to increase your card limit whilst you are still employed. It is going to be far easier to be granted a higher limit with a regular salary coming in than making a request when you are self employed.

Credit cards are ideal for short term or emergency funding especially if you know exactly when you are expecting funds to pay off your bill. Although you can pay only the prescribed minimum amount each month it's wise not to treat your card as your sole means of finance – it should be used for emergency purposes only. Card debt can be a crippling long term burden and with the cost involved it is not an option to be considered lightly; credit cards are the most expensive form of debt (up to 20% or in some cases more) and unless managed correctly can turn into a financial maelstrom. But if you need a cash lump sum to kick start your business, get your expansion off the ground or to fill a short cash flow gap and you are comfortable you can pay it off within a few months, then it's an alternative source of finance worth considering ... as a last resort!

Business Grants

Business grants are available for a wide range of general and specific industries, sectors and purposes. Grant agencies will usually only provide a portion of your requirement and they will want to see a contribution from you as evidence of your commitment to succeed. However, grants can be useful in filling a funding gap and banks will consider a grant as matched funding for facilities they may provide.

Just as with requesting bank finance there are processes to go through and application forms to complete. Whilst the amount of detail required is not usually as onerous as that requested by banks, to ensure you are successful you need to present a professional image and a lot of the information contained in this book will help you prepare a winning proposal.

For more information on the type of grants available and eligibility criteria visit your local Business Link office or website - **www.**

businesslink.gov.uk, or call your local Council to check what grant schemes are currently available.

Business Angels and Venture Capitalists

These groups are external financiers who are looking to take shares in your business in return for funding. Perhaps the best known angels are the entrepreneurs who make up the Dragons' Den. They can operate with different agendas and styles of doing business so choose with care.

Angels and venture capitalists usually go where banks fear to tread, so higher risk start ups and technology/IT-based businesses are more likely to go down this path.

Business Angels

Business Angels are wealthy individuals, usually retired or successful business people in their own right, who are looking to support businesses with amounts between £10,000 and £750,000. They can act on their own or through a syndicate and primarily look for investments in start ups, early stage businesses or those in expansion mode.

Angels are either philanthropic in their aims i.e. genuinely wanting to help fellow entrepreneurs or they approach their investment strictly from the perspective of their expected financial return. Because of this mix of expectations, finding an angel who fits both your criteria and theirs can take many months so don't plan on a quick close to your search.

In exchange for an investment in a business they would typically want an equity stake (a shareholding) and usually a degree of hands-on involvement depending both on their wishes and that of the entrepreneur they are supporting. The angel will have vast business experience and so are useful people to have on board; they can bring fresh ideas and challenge the way a business is run.

However, with an angel as an investor in your business you will have to accept an element of loss of control, if not day-to-day control but at least in terms of strategy and business direction. You need to balance this downside against your desire for funding, especially if you can't get support from the bank.

Business angels will look at your funding request using the same general assessment criteria as a bank, so if you have approached a bank you can expect a request for the same information and perhaps even the same final answer! As entrepreneurs in their own right though they are likely to be much less risk averse than banks and they may be able to see something in your business that the bank can't and so be more willing to invest.

More information on Business Angels can be found at www.bbaa. org.uk which is the trade association for the sector. You can also find an angel at **www.angelinvestmentnetwork.co.uk**

Venture Capitalists

Venture Capitalists, or VCs as they are known, will want an equity stake in return for their investment with a very clear exit route and specific exit timeframe, typically between three and five years. Whilst smaller VCs may consider investments as low as £50,000, most start at £2,000,000.

Unlike angels, VCs tend not to get involved at the day-to-day level but as a result the initial investment review is very intense and robust to ensure the right investment decision is being made.

Whilst this all may sound rather daunting, having a recognised VC on board will certainly open doors and lead to potential further investment.

If you are in a high risk sector or looking to raise large sums then this route is worth investigating.

You can find out more from The British Private Equity and Venture Capital Association (BVCA) at **www.bvca.co.uk/PEVCExplained**

Debtors

Many business owners don't understand the importance of cash flow and the positive or negative impact it can have on their business. One key element of how cash moves within your business is the velocity of your debtor collection (the speed with which you collect your debtors). How quickly you can turn debtors back into cash determines how much you have to re-invest back into stock, which can then be turned into goods to sell. The more cash you have available the more product you can put into the market.

The quality of your debtor portfolio is also vital – a poor quality debtor will leave you constantly chasing for payment and so wasting valuable time. A poor quality client could eventually lead to an unpaid debt the size of which could put serious pressure on your finances. Focusing on giving credit terms to the better quality businesses is an excellent preventative measure against a cash crisis.

So how can you release cash from your debtor portfolio?

Let's say you currently give your customers 45 days in which to pay up and your debtor book totals £50,000. That is £50,000 tied up which you cannot use; all you can do is sit back and wait for a cheque to arrive. Let's say you have an expansion plan which needs an additional stock of £10,000; you don't have it so you go to the bank cap in hand. But what if you could reduce the credit period to 30 days? That would put cash into your hands 15 days quicker than before, thereby releasing that additional cash to work for you in different ways ... all at no additional interest cost.

A strategy to reduce the number of days' credit given can take a while to implement and there are customer sensitivities to take into account. If you have planned your new cash requirement well in advance you can slowly migrate customers on to the new credit terms so potentially avoiding a grovelling session with the bank.

It may be difficult, though, to move a well established and loyal client base over to your new terms. Your larger and reliable payers are likely to resist any change which is detrimental to their cash flow position. If you don't wish to put future business at risk you could resolve to implement the tighter credit terms for new customers only.

This strategy can take time before the benefits are seen, so what if you are looking for a quick injection of cash? If control of your debtor book is not that good then it's possible you have some late payers hidden in there or even clients who have dropped off your radar and not paid at all. Examine your debtor book; go through your invoices to see who is late paying you and who seems to have forgotten you exist! Getting tough with old debtors is akin to lifting up the sofa cushions to see if you can find a hidden £1 coin ... yes, you know there's probably some loose change buried in cushions but there are better things to do and so you do nothing!

It's the same with debtors you have dealt with for years - you know they'll pay eventually so why chase them? When times are tough you have to start talking tough. If administration and pushing clients for payment is not your strong point consider outsourcing it. Cash is what keeps your business going and it's too important to treat lightly.

"Using a Debt Collector doesn't have the same stigma that was once associated with it several years ago.

Debt Collectors are specialists in dealing with delinquent accounts, and the causes behind them, leaving entrepreneurs to get on with the job of running their business. We know the tricks of the trade which will get invoices paid; after all, this is our job and we do it on a daily basis!

By using a trusted and researched Debt Collection company, your time will be freed up to concentrate on your business. Debt Collectors have no issues, nor will they get embarrassed by asking for payment. They have no emotional tie to the money as you would and we will remember to persistently chase the debtor for payment. Would you have the time to do that AND run your own business?

You need to have a plan on how you are going to tackle late payers and then stick to it! It is no good threatening to take certain steps in your first letter if you don't follow that action up, because subsequent letters will mean nothing! A Debt Collection company takes away this hassle.

Using a Debt Collector is akin to outsourcing your IT requirements ... if you can't fix it, call in the experts."

Steve White, Thornbury Collections Limited, www.thornburycollections.co.uk

Another strategy is to offer your clients a discount of, say, 5% if they either pay at the time of ordering or at least upon receipt of invoice. Whilst the idea of giving a discount may not appeal to you, think about what you can do with 95% of your money today as opposed to 100% in say 60 days ... I'm sure you could turn that 95% into something much larger during that 60 days?

We will look more in depth into cash flow later in the book. For the moment you need to understand that by positively influencing your debtor book you can release more cash into your business so allowing you to bypass the bank – a quicker and cheaper option.

Invoice Finance - Discounting and Factoring

Another way to make your debtor book work harder for you is to look at raising finance directly against the money owed to you. Invoice financing is a way of improving your cash flow in a very structured way by taking out a short term loan against your invoices. The popularity of this source of financing has increased over the years, especially amongst the banks, following a court ruling which changed the way banks could look at debtors as security (more of this later on).

There are two types of invoice financing

- Invoice Discounting
- Invoice Factoring

The distinction between the two services is as simple as who owns the final invoice collection process. With invoice discounting, the financier will advance an agreed percentage of the invoice immediately upon presentation but the debt collection responsibility lies with you; it's up to you to chase the debtor for payment. Once payment has been made and confirmed by you the financier will send you the balance due, less their charges (effectively the equivalent of bank interest).

Factoring is slightly different in that you pass on the debt collection responsibility to the financier; they have essentially bought the invoice off you so it's down to them to collect payment.

Whilst the end result is the same the key decision to make as to which option to go for is whether you wish your clients to know that, for example, you are factoring your debts. If you chose the factoring option your client will know this because the collection is done by the factoring company. Some business owners think this implies they have a cash flow problem and don't want their clients thinking this.

Discounting means your client has no idea that you have raised cash against his invoice because he still deals directly with you.

The advantage of financing your business via either route is that as your sales increase you don't have to go back to the bank to renegotiate a higher overdraft limit. As your working capital requirement increases all you have to do is to continue sending in the invoices.

Most discounters and factors will offer a bad debt insurance which covers you should the debtor fail to pay – very useful for total peace of mind.

This service, which is provided by nearly all High Street banks and other specialised providers, is a good way of keep the cash flowing within your business.

For more information on both discounting and factoring visit the Asset Based Finance Association - **www.abfa.org.uk**

Creditors

Creditors are the flip side of your debtors. These are the people and businesses you owe money to. Creditors also have a positive and negative impact on cash flow and again you could avoid going to the bank by re-looking at your credit payment terms.

Firstly, if you need a quick cash boost you could approach your main creditors and request a delay in payment. Extending your creditor terms by an extra 15 or 30 days, assuming your debtor collection days have remained the same, will give you the cash you need to kick start your plan. This assumes, of course, that your expansion plan will start bringing the cash in quickly enough to settle your creditors on the due date. Extending terms will give you some breathing space but it's not a long term solution.

If the first option is not feasible then the second option is to agree revised payment terms for all new purchases going forward thereby providing certainty of cash flow.

Your ability to implement one of these options is down to your relationship with your suppliers. If you have a track record of late or slow payment then your suppliers are likely to be less keen to support you. So before you go down this route think carefully about your track record and reputation – you don't want to be walking away with your tail between your legs.

Stock

In busy times it is too easy to become blind to the growing pile of boxes in your warehouse or storeroom. If you are the type who becomes distracted by the 'business of doing business' then before you realise it you could have thousands tied up in 'must have' stock which was a Christmas best seller ... three years ago.

Having money tied up in obsolete or slow moving stock is an inefficient use of resources and having that cash released into the system could be the difference between going to the bank for help or not.

Here are some actions you can take:

- Sell 'dead' stock at any price – don't tell me it's worth three grand and so you must hang on ... it's not; if someone had wanted it why has it been stuck in the corner for the last four years?

- Hold a sale to shift slow moving stock to quickly raise cash

- Review the fast and slow moving items so you can adjust your purchasing patterns or decisions accordingly

Other Options to Consider

Some of the other ways of raising cash, either internally or externally of the business, include:

- Selling obsolete machinery or equipment
- Selling machinery or equipment which is not being full utilised and so unlikely to be missed
- Selling spare land
- Sub-letting unused parts of your building or office
- Sale and leaseback of your premises
- If you have a SIPP (Self Invested Personal Pension) talk to your broker or provider as you may be able to raise cash against it

If All Else Fails ...

If, after having been through this extensive list of alternatives, you have no choice but to get on bended knees, begging bowl in hand, and go to your nearest bank, there is one very important point for you to understand ...

The bank is not a venture capitalist; it is not there to help fund experiments, finance research projects, or to take your concept to the marketable product stage. This is risk capital which either comes from your savings or a private investor.

With that said, let's move on to the first part of your journey to the Bank Manager's door ... your Business Plan.

OH NO! HE WANTS A BUSINESS PLAN

You've been through all the alternative funding options but there is nothing else to do ... you have to go and visit the bank. So armed with your great idea, which you're sure will be a winner, you jot down a few notes, jump in the car and head off to see the Bank Manager.

But disaster! Your interview lasts all of 5 minutes!

Whilst the Manager nodded sagely as you launched into a long-winded summary of why you need £50,000, the only thing he said was, "So let me see your Business Plan. You have got one haven't you?"

A Business Plan? You abruptly tell him that you didn't see the point in wasting valuable time doing one of those when you could be planning your launch ... and at that point he abruptly tells you to leave and don't darken his door until you have a Business Plan.

And for many business people, at this point, their wonderful idea starts falling apart.

If you're in business, and you want to borrow money, one fact of life you'll need to know is that most Bank Managers today will want to see a Business Plan. That said, if you're lucky enough to have banked at the same bank for many years, with an extremely strong relationship and a superb track record, then you may get away with not having to prepare one. For the rest of us, a Business Plan is a must, especially if you are a start up which is considered to be one of the riskiest businesses to lend to, an untouchable, but a Business Plan will help give you a much needed edge. During the boom years it might have been possible to get funding purely on the back of an idea but in today's climate a Plan is now essential.

If your bank hasn't asked for a Business Plan, and they seem happy to go with the grubby piece of paper ripped out of your children's school book, you should not breathe a sigh of relief. Firstly, you should seriously consider spending time preparing a plan anyway, because there are a number of benefits for both you and the business which we will explore later. Secondly, if your Manager hasn't asked for a Business Plan ... consider changing banks!

> *"I feel one of the secrets is to over prepare. Banks still like to see your version of war and peace, and they need to know you are prepared to do what it takes to succeed.*
>
> *Many years ago I wanted a business loan, and prepared a full Business Plan with a cash flow forecast, set of accounts and lots of supporting information. Was I disappointed when the Manager took a cursory look at my endeavours? Well yes ... however I did get the loan which was the objective."*
> **Deborah Rees, Lean Synergies,**
> **www.leansynergies.co.uk**

But where do you start? When it comes to writing Business Plans, many business owners haven't got a clue. It's not their fault. I've seen lots of attempts and the majority don't do justice to the business because writing about themselves and their business is not something done every day.

No need to worry though. In this chapter we are going to provide you with an overview of what goes into a sound and workable Business Plan.

If you are totally in the dark, let's start by looking at exactly what a Business Plan is.

What is a Business Plan?

If you are planning to start up in business or planning to expand your existing business, you'll no doubt have a mental list of how you'll go about it and a picture in your mind of what a great success it will be! That's fine; all great ideas and businesses start with the owner's vision but try explaining that vision to someone else and at the same time making sure nothing is missed out. In a verbal presentation, a few omissions to the description of your grand plan could be fatal.

It's not easy, especially under the pressure of an interview, to remember all the points which need to be covered. How many times have you finished a conversation only to remember 10 minutes later that you forgot to mention a crucial aspect of your scheme? Without having a well prepared agenda to follow, talking from the top of your head to ensure all angles are covered is harder than you think.

In presenting your business case without the support of a Business Plan you require first class communication skills and sadly, in many cases, people don't possess this skill, leaving a very confused Bank Manager. This is where a Business Plan can make all the difference.

So what exactly is a Business Plan?

- One document containing everything a complete stranger needs to know about your business
- A structured and logical framework which, when followed, ensures that all aspects of the business are clearly set out
- It reflects the owner's dreams and ambitions and sets out his short, medium and long term goals and objectives
- A document which can be used to monitor progress against business goals and objectives

A Business Plan must sell your passion, vision and commitment, all of which must come across strongly enough to convince someone to invest in your business venture, whether it is new or well established.

Once your Bank Manager puts the Plan down, you want him to be so enthused that he immediately picks up the phone and calls you in for a chat – with a big fat cheque sitting in his drawer payable to you! Your Plan needs to be this powerful … powerful enough for him to say the one word you want to hear, 'Yes'.

Why It Pays To Put In the Effort

If, by outlining what a Business Plan is, I haven't convinced you why you should spend some of your valuable time writing one, here are the main benefits for both you and your business:

- No matter how good a communicator you are, you will never be able to convey your vision for the business as successfully as a perfectly written Business Plan. It provides a clear understanding as to what you want to achieve. It allows you to express your ideas in a clearer manner.

- A Business Plan will help convince both you and a potential investor of your project's feasibility and viability. There's nothing like having all the facts in front of you to clarify the key issues.

- There's no getting away from the fact that a business owner who plans ahead comes across as being more ambitious and more focused. A well prepared Business Plan demonstrates you have vision and that you know what you want.

- With numerous ideas floating around in your mind, the pitfalls or stumbling blocks to success are never that visible. A mind buzzing and full of ideas will rarely achieve clarity. A Business Plan forces you to put your ideas down in writing and in an orderly manner. The result of this could be you going in a completely different direction than you initially thought of, or even abandoning your idea altogether. Not a pleasant thought, but which would you prefer? The loss of your hard earned capital or the opportunity to re-think your idea?

- It is an ideal tool to monitor progress against the objectives you have set yourself. By checking progress against your Plan, you will be able to spot if you are moving away from your original vision and so you'll know what has to be put right. Imagine if you didn't have this check in place; an unnoticed change in direction or a slippage in achieving your objectives, if left uncorrected for too long, could be fatal to your business. On the other hand, it may transpire that a shift from your original vision could be a better alternative. At least recognising this change allows you to adjust your direction in a planned, structured and controlled manner.

- Every action you take has a consequence, and a Plan helps make these consequences clearer. Being aware of the possible effect of your chosen direction allows you to plan ahead, leaving you better able to cope with whatever the world of entrepreneurship can throw at you. This is one thing that "mental planning" would not achieve.

- Putting your thoughts on paper may make you realise that you need to do more research into the demand for your product or service, for example. It could also highlight that more investigation on your competitor's products or services is needed. Additional research could help avoid a potentially costly mistake or even uncover a hidden advantage, which you had not seen before!

- A Plan will guide you as to how much money is needed to make an idea work. You may have a rough figure of what you'll have to commit, but until you do a Cash Flow Forecast you may not realise that short-term support will be required, in addition to a loan for your equipment.

- A Business Plan will help you get funding. One of the main reasons banks or investors turn down requests for support is the lack of information to assist in making an informed decision. A Business Plan will make an investor feel much more at ease and so more able to say yes.

- By the time you have finished writing your Business Plan you will have a total understanding of your business - its strengths and weaknesses, the environment it operates in, what could potentially go wrong, and what you can do to ensure your success. Doing your planning on the back of an envelope is not going to achieve this.

You should realise by now that it's essential to have a Business Plan; it could be the difference between success and that dreaded "f" word - failure! It's all about understanding the importance of planning ahead. You would never entertain the idea of driving to a place you've never been to before without first planning your route. Yet, this is exactly what many business owners do; they blindly start up in business or seek to expand their existing one, with no thought about the possible pit-falls and no logical approach to the whole planning process.

For many start ups or expanding businesses, it's head down, full steam ahead and no time to look for the dangers ahead.

Spend time putting your thoughts on paper in a structured and logical manner. It will pay you dividends when you come to apply to the bank.

You're Not On Your Own - There Is Help!

Many people fall at the first hurdle and don't produce a Plan because they haven't the faintest clue where to start. They sit down with a pen and paper and 3 hours later all they have is a bin full of scrap paper. There is no excuse for this to happen. If you have never put a Business Plan together, you don't have to struggle on your own because there is plenty of support out there to help you write a blockbuster of a Plan.

Your Team

Don't ignore the people who know as much about your business as you do - your staff. Enlist their help and use all the knowledge they possess. It's usual to find that in some cases they have a more in-depth knowledge about specific areas of the business than you!

Bring together the key people in your business and explain to them what you are planning to do, and that you need their help in compiling a Business Plan. Allocate specific parts of the Plan to the people who have the right skills: sales and marketing to your sales and marketing people; production issues to your production team etc. Tell them that you need a complete overview of their contribution to the business: how their department works, how they interact with the rest of the business, their strengths and weaknesses.

Don't overlook the power of co-opting your staff in helping to complete your Plan. There is no better way to achieve "buy-in" to your vision and strategy than getting your team involved. If your business is big enough, you may even want to extend the involvement to all staff by getting feedback from them through think tanks or focus groups.

If you are successful in obtaining finance then, having contributed, your people will be ready to forge ahead because they know what you are looking for; they are aware of the bigger picture and where the business is heading. Getting team involvement is a powerful strategy.

Accountants

Ask for help from an accountant; he will have seen many Plans and so can provide practical advice, particularly where Profit and Loss and Cash Flow Forecasts are concerned. If you don't feel comfortable with figures or you don't have an accountant within your business, then it would be wise to seek help in compiling these figures; after all, the bank is going to make some very important decisions based on these forecasts, so they have to be as accurate as possible.

However, don't underestimate the benefits of doing the forecasts yourself. This exercise will give you a very good understanding of how your business works from a financial perspective; you'll realise the importance of managing cash properly and the effect a rapidly increasing or decreasing turnover can have on your cash requirement. In addition, doing the figures yourself will give you the motivation to monitor your performance on a regular basis. So, before going to seek help from an accountant, have a go at putting the figures together yourself. You can find sample templates online to complete. It will eat into your evenings or weekends but you'll find it's time well spent!

Once you have finished the forecasts, you can still ask your accountant to review them to ensure that you're not totally mad! He can give you a formal 'stamp of approval' to include in your Business Plan.

If you don't have an accountant, speak to other business people and get a recommendation from them as to whom to use. A recommendation can save you many hours of phone calls and interviews.

The Bank

You may think that the bank would not wish to spend time talking through your idea, but don't forget that they are on the lookout for good business, so it's in their interest to get in early before any other bank does. The bank's aim is to build a relationship with you, so they will be pleased to provide their thoughts on any expansion plans. If you don't get this support from your Manager, move on and find someone else!

Getting the bank involved early on means you can pick their brains and get their initial views, before you make any irreversible decisions. You may think this is a bit odd but being pointed in the right direction may save you time later. For example, by seeking their early thoughts, you may get the impression, or even direct feedback, that the bank is not keen on your idea, or you're in a sector that they are currently not supporting. This will be a very clear message that you may be better off placing your request with another bank.

If this is your first time in business, or the first Plan you are writing, asking someone to go through the key issues with you will provide advice and a number of tips, which aren't necessarily included in any bank booklets or brochures. The advantage of this approach is it won't cost you a penny and you are establishing an immediate relationship with the person who will be reviewing your Plan.

However, if you do go down this route, don't use it as an opportunity to "sell" your idea; it's too early and your Manager may feel that he's being pushed into a corner and forced into making a decision by default. In other words he has given so much advice that he can't say no to the request (not a bad idea but a bit underhand!) The key is finding a suitable balance.

Business Advice Agencies

If you can't afford to employ help, go and see your local business advice centre or agency. These are Government funded bodies whose sole purpose is to give free advice to startups and established businesses looking to expand. They will help you in all aspects of your Plan and point you in the right direction for further help.

Most agencies run periodic courses and seminars on how to prepare Business Plans and a variety of other related topics, so a visit would be worthwhile.

Business Colleagues, Local Chambers Of Commerce, Chambers of Trade and Networking Groups

These are organisations comprising local business people who get together on a regular basis to share ideas and experiences, hold seminars and trade fairs. You may think that people already in business, especially in the same industry or sector as you, would not want to help someone else start up in business or expand in case it damages their own firm. However, this is far from the case.

All entrepreneurs know what it's like during the early days in business or the problems encountered in trying to grow an existing one. They will be more than willing to share their experiences and give some general advice. You'll be surprised at how generous some business people can be.

Books

There are numerous books on how to prepare Business Plans. Each of them has something different to add, so buy a few and pick up some of the key points.

Take a visit to your local library. As well as books on how to put a Plan together they may have information relating to your line of business, which could be useful in gathering background facts to bring your Plan to life.

Hiring Professional Business Plan Writers

If you genuinely can't make the time or have other very compelling reasons for not writing a Plan yourself you may want to think about seeking assistance by hiring a professional Business Plan writer.

If you are interested in acquiring the services of a professional Business Plan writer, you will have a number of different options. One of those options is to find someone locally. Dealing with a local writer is great if you want to meet face-to-face. The only problem you may find is that not all areas of your country have professional Business Plan writers available. This means you may have to turn to the Internet for assistance. Online, there are a large number of professional writers who specialise in creating, writing, or reviewing Business Plans. Using your favourite search engine, search for the terms 'business plan writer', 'business plan consultant', 'hire business plan writer' and you'll find a bewildering number. If you really want a local resource then add into your search term your area, region or city. This will significantly reduce the number of hits you get back.

If you are short of time or lacking in the skill then hiring a writer is a good solution, but don't forget that writing your own Business Plan is the best way to understand your business. You must make every effort to write the majority of the Plan yourself; delegating it to someone else, whilst having advantages, can negatively impact on the feeling of ownership, which is essential for Business Plans.

Business Plan Software

There are a number of software programs out there that can, for a reasonable price, easily prepare a Business Plan. These programs are worth considering and can take some of the pain out of writing a Business Plan for the first time.

Unlike hiring a professional writer, you research and input the data into the program so the element of ownership of the Plan and its content is maintained, making the software a reasonable compromise between the do-it-yourself and professional writer approach.

What to Include In Your Plan

Let's assume you have decided to have a stab at writing your Plan by yourself. Many entrepreneurs, who are asked to put together a Business Plan for the first time, end up staring at a blank page for hours, scratching their heads as to where to start. However, with a framework as a guide, the task does become easier.

There are 3 main areas to address when developing your Plan, each of them having specific issues to focus on.

Where you are now

- An outline of your business
- Your location and premises
- Your products or services
- The market you operate in
- Your customers
- The competition
- Staffing and equipment
- Financial information – summary of last three years Financial Statements

Where you intend to be

- Future business objectives
- Outline of your request
- Why you need the finance

How you are going to get there

- Marketing plan
- Additional resources required
- Your contribution
- Security offered
- Financial projections - Profit and Loss, Balance Sheet and Cash Flow Forecast
- A clear demonstration of ability to service the proposed debt

Supporting Information

- Appendices

Just by following this framework you can immediately see how your Plan will take shape.

In preparing a request for finance don't be tempted to skip the writing of a Business Plan. It is an essential step which is not only useful for the bank but also for you. The research and writing involved will leave you better prepared and with a greater understanding of the issues you may face going forward.

THE INTERVIEW - YES, YOU'RE GOING TO HAVE TO TALK TO HIM!

Having prepared your Business Plan, you may think this should be sufficient for the bank to make a decision on whether to support you or not. Unfortunately this is not the case. A Business Plan has one vital element missing - you!

A Plan cannot capture your personality nor convey your drive, passion and energy. Your Bank Manager will want to see you face-to-face so that the human side of your business can be assessed.

For many entrepreneurs, the idea of having to talk about their business to an "outsider" fills them with dread! Thoughts such as these could be going through your mind:

- "I can never talk with any confidence. I become a gibbering wreck."
- "I know what I want to say but I can't express my ideas as I want them."
- "Whenever I talk in public I always come across as being nervous."
- "How can I do justice to my vision and my business?"

These are common fears initially held by all entrepreneurs, especially when obtaining funding for an important project. But why? And how can you be better prepared?

Why People Feel Nervous In Presenting Plans

First of all, let's consider why people find the idea of selling themselves and their business a daunting task.

Lack of Confidence

Some people just don't feel confident when talking in public. You may not consider communicating on a one-to-one basis as talking in public, but it is. Outside of your own "self-talk" (conversations you have in your mind) and within your own home, all conversations are essentially public speeches.

Lack of Preparation

Most of us have experienced this, in that if you have done no or little preparation then this will show through in any stressful situation. A make-or-break presentation to your bank can be classed as one of those stress moments!

Lack of preparation includes not knowing the ins-and-outs of your business idea or Business Plan and not anticipating the type of questions you'll be asked during the interview. It's comparable to going into an examination and knowing deep down that you haven't put the effort in - do you remember that feeling?

Poor Communication Skills

Some people feel they can never communicate their ideas in a clear and coherent manner; their thoughts are jumbled up and are not in any order; words and explanation of concepts come out in a confusing way. As a result their body language and voice begins to reflect this uneasiness, which leads to even more mental anguish.

And so the cycle continues ... ever downward!

Poor Self Image

Some people don't see the interview as a meeting of equals in which both parties want a successful outcome. They see the Manager as some kind of ogre, someone who takes pleasure in making someone squirm! OK, I'm sure there are some bankers like this, but not all!

An enduring image of such torture can stay with you right up to the start of an interview, dominating your thoughts and making the whole process a complete disaster! A poor self image can be devastating to an effective presentation.

Lack of Focus and Planning

On the day of the interview, some people try to do a thousand and one other things before going along to the bank. What happens? They get stressed out because something has not gone to plan - the man who was coming to repair the washing machine didn't turn up until an hour after the agreed time; he forgot that the car needs refuelling and this adds 10 minutes to the journey time; a friend turns up at the house and they don't have the courage to tell her to go, so there's an hour wasted!

By the time they get to the bank, their heart is beating faster than that of a marathon runner and their mind is a complete blank! They haven't realised that the day has one purpose only ... that of seeing the Bank Manager. Nothing else should matter.

All these unplanned diversions and delusions can take your mind off mentally preparing for the important task ahead.

Do any of these situations sound familiar? If so, what can you do to put yourself in a better frame of mind?

What You Can Do To Prepare Yourself

You have to accept that if you want the Bank to say yes to your superb business idea you are going to have to spend time preparing for the interview. The chat with the Manager is your only chance to really sell yourself and your idea. It's rare that you'll get a second chance with the same Manager or bank. Once they say no, it's unlikely they will change their mind, so you have to get it right first time. Don't deny yourself the opportunity presented by making the simple mistake of being unprepared.

There's only one way to get the success you deserve and that's to put in the preparation to prepare the perfect pitch and then **practise**, **practise** and **practise** again!

Let's look at what you can do to secure a head start and make this whole process much less stressful.

The 9 Steps to Preparing For an Interview

In helping to prepare for your interview there are a number of things you can do to improve your chances of a successful outcome. Here are the 9 steps you can take to prepare yourself.

Step One - Have Belief in Your Future Success

Before someone else can believe in you, you have to believe in yourself. You must absolutely have no doubt in your own mind that you *will* succeed in setting up your business or moving your current business forward. It's not about what you believe you are now but what you believe you can be in the future. You may have little in the way of money or assets now but you have to believe that in the future you will have all these things (if this is how you define success). People, and this includes your Bank Manager, support and follow the person who *believes* in what he is saying.

I have lost count of the number of times someone meekly opened an interview with the immortal line, "I know you probably can't help me but ..."

Quick answer – yes you're right; I can't help you! My thought would be that if you can't sell yourself to me how on earth do you sell your business??

So, before trying to persuade someone else to invest in you, ensure you believe you can do it. This unshakeable belief in yourself and your idea *must* come over during the interview. Leave the Manager in no doubt about how much faith you have in yourself.

Step Two - Know Your Business Plan Inside Out

If you have organised yourself properly and sent in a copy of your Plan in advance, the Manager will have spent time going through it before the interview. He may now have a list of questions or areas to clarify to give him a better understanding of certain aspects of your business.

To deal confidently with these questions you have to know your Plan inside out. In view of the time constraints people are under these days, it's possible that the Manager may only have skimmed through your Plan. (What! After all your work? After all those hours? Yep, it's a fact of life I'm afraid!) The answers to his queries, of course, may actually be contained in the Plan. If this does happen, don't lose your cool or answer with an "attitude". Use this as an opportunity to demonstrate your knowledge of your Plan. Think how professional and organised you'll look when you tell him to turn to page 10 and he'll find the answer to his question right there! If nothing else, it will make him feel humble!

The Manager may also deliberately feign ignorance, knowing full well that the answer is contained in the Plan. Take your financial information, for example. A good business person will know all his key numbers off pat. Learn your numbers – sales, gross profit, net profit etc. Nothing impresses more than an entrepreneur who knows his figures.

Knowing your Plan and its contents also means that during the interview you're not going to contradict what you included in it! You have to be consistent. If you say something which doesn't tally with what you stated on paper, what do you think will go through the Manager's mind? "Does this person know what he's doing? They obviously don't have a clear direction or focus for the business if they keep changing their mind."

During this whole process you want to avoid throwing any doubt about your ability to deliver upon your Plan. Knowing your Plan will demonstrate that you are meticulous, organised and consistent … the type of person a banker really likes.

Step Three - Let Someone Else Read Your Business Plan

When you are engrossed in putting something together you become blind to the obvious mistakes. When editing your Plan your mind sometimes sees what you *intended* to write, not what you *actually* wrote. If you miss it once, the more times you read your Plan, the more often your mind tells you it's perfect.

The solution is to give your Plan to someone to proofread for you. They have not been labouring over it for hours and so will very quickly spot mistakes, which in hindsight were obvious!

Another common problem when putting pen to paper is that we don't put down our thoughts as clearly as they are set out in our mind. You know what you want to say but when it's down on paper it just doesn't come across in a coherent manner. If someone else proofreads your Plan they will quickly spot sections which may not make sense. They will be reading it for the first time, as will the Bank Manager, and they probably know just as little about your business or your idea as he will. They will be able to say whether you have clearly expressed yourself and whether you have been able to convey your commitment to the project.

Step Four - Put Yourself in the Manager's Shoes

One effective way of preparing for the interview is to imagine yourself as the Bank Manager. A daunting thought I know but bear with me!

Imagine you are interviewing yourself and reading your Business Plan for the first time; pretend you know absolutely nothing about you or your business. What would you ask of yourself? What would you want to know? What is likely to confuse an "outsider" about your business? What questions would you ask to get a better understanding of the business? What challenging questions would you ask yourself?

You have to get inside a Bank Manager's mind so you can prepare well-researched and well-presented answers to his likely questions. It's all back to being professional in your presentation, demonstrating that you know your business and that you are worthy of support. You won't give this impression if you haven't spent time thinking of possible questions you could be asked and preparing the answers in advance.

Banker's favourite questions are "What if......" ones:

- "What if your supplier fails you?"
- "What if the price of your raw materials goes up by 10%?"
- "What if you lose your number one customer?"

- "What if one of your critically important employees leaves?"

What would you want to know if you were in his chair? The list of questions could be endless and there is no way you can pre-empt all of them but at least you will be better prepared than the majority who will sit in front of him.

If you find this exercise difficult to do, ask someone else to come up with likely questions. Choose someone who, like your Manager, does not have an intimate knowledge of your business or your background. Ask him or her to read your Plan and list as many questions as he can think of, just as if he was preparing to interview you. You may be surprised with what he'll come up with, issues which you thought were simple or very clearly stated in your Plan but are not so clear to a third party.

Commit time to doing this exercise. It will pay you great dividends.

Step Five - Prepare Your Pitch

You have to see the interview as your sales pitch. This is your chance of selling yourself, your idea and your business. An actor's job is to go on the stage and make people believe he is the person he's portraying. He does this by thorough preparation, which includes learning his script, how to stand and sit, how to put across true meaning and feeling in what he says.

All of this is achieved through understanding and learning his script. You have to think like an actor. Your script is your Business Plan. Spend time to come up with questions you may be asked, so all that remains for you to do is practise your delivery.

The Manager will have your Plan in front of him and, hopefully, he will have read it, but he is going to want to hear you pitch your ideas to him; he doesn't just want to learn about your plans from a few pages of A4 paper. After all, he is lending to you as an individual, not to a Business Plan! Reading a Plan does not give you a feel for the real person behind the business. The reader needs to see and 'feel' the business through you.

To be ready for this you have to prepare a script, which sells you and the business. Take each aspect of the Plan and come up with a list of the main points you wish to put across. Against each point, write down some of your key thoughts and then play around with how you would phrase them. You don't want to ramble on and put the Manager to sleep, so make your points exciting, interesting and not too long.

Your pitch should also include the strengths and weaknesses of both you and your business. Whilst your pitch is about presenting the positive aspects of your business and the future opportunities available to you, it is also the time to acknowledge the negatives. Any experienced Banker will quickly pick up on the flaws in your Plan or a questionable aspect of your background which could impact your business, so be up front and honest and weave this into your pitch.

Two of the key elements of your presentation, which have to be thoroughly prepared, are your opening and closing remarks. These have to concisely sum up what you want from the bank and portray confidence in your ability to achieve and deliver on the plans you have made. The words used and the presentation has to be upbeat and positive. People tend to better remember the first and last thing they hear, so make your opening and closing remarks powerful and compelling. Remember what I said earlier, whatever you do, don't start the interview with an opening line such as,

"I know you probably can't help me but.........."

This is weak and uninspiring. Start off with something along the lines of, "Thank you for seeing me today. I trust you have had the chance to review my Business Plan. As you know, I am looking for a loan to ......"

Similarly, your closing remarks have to be prepared in advance and rehearsed. Try something along the lines of, "Thank you very much for your time. I'm sure you can see that I'm fully committed to making this venture succeed. If you want to know more, give me a call. If not, then I look forwarding to receiving your answer soon."

A weak close such as, "Oh I do hope you can help me", is not going to get you very far! Your closing statement has to be upbeat, positive, determined and demonstrate that you are raring to go.

Knowing what to say and how to say it will make you look professional and worthy of support and that's your aim. Someone who stumbles over their words and whose sentences are full of "ums" and "ahs" will not impress. A salesperson that has a prepared sales pitch will reap the benefits, and so it will be for you if you have a prepared pitch. The key is finding the balance between being perceived as weak and aggressive or pushy!

Step Six - Prepare Your Questions

You don't want to let the Manager dominate the interview with all his questions; you should join in as well. After all, the purpose of the meeting is not only for him to assess you; it's also an opportunity for you to assess him, which is why you have to prepare some questions to fire at him.

There are a number of good reasons why you should ask questions during the interview:

• Asking questions shows you can think for yourself and that you are confident enough to challenge something you don't understand.

- Questioning demonstrates you have an enquiring mind, a quality which is important in business.

- Asking questions is an excellent way of checking the listener's understanding of what you've told them; it gives you the chance to put right any misunderstandings or misconceptions they may have.

- Asking questions is a good way of building rapport.

- Don't forget that this is going to be your chance to decide whether you want to do business with this person. Having a Bank Manager whom you can't get on with is not good for your business. You need someone whom you can ring up and feel comfortable to talk to, someone who comes across as being genuinely interested in your business. If you don't feel comfortable with him this will reflect in your attitude and this is not a basis for a good working relationship. Asking questions will put your mind at rest and help you make a decision as to which bank you'll go with.

- You should have questions about the cost of the overdraft or loan; how long it will take to set up, the rate of interest, and the fees.

- Questions can be used as another method of positively manipulating the Manager. One technique to use in your questioning is to build an assumption into the question, for example:

  o "How long would it take before my loan is available?"

  o "Would I be able to pay lump sums off my loan without any penalty?"

o "What interest rate are you going to charge me?"

> You can see that in these questions there is an in-built assumption that the loan will be agreed! A bit bold but on the other hand it again demonstrates self-confidence.

> However, some Managers can spot this technique! Whenever I had it used on me, I responded by saying,

> "Well, assuming your loan/overdraft is agreed ...."

> This ensures there is no misunderstanding and puts the other person on notice that he can't assume anything!

You can't rely on quickness of mind to come up with all the relevant questions on the spot, hence my advice to take time before the interview to come up with a list.

In addition to the questions already shown above, here are some 'non assumptive' questions you can ask.

- "What do you know about the industry we are in?"
- "Do you have the ability to make decisions on requests to borrow money, or are you answerable to someone else?" or if you feel this a little bit 'in your face' you could ask more tactfully, "How exactly does your loan process work?" and move on from there.
- "Will you be available to call if I have any problems, or will I end up in some dreadful Call Centre?"
- "Developing a relationship and working with someone who understands my business is important to me. How long are you going to be in this job before you move on?"

The answers to these questions will provide you with more information on the person who is going to be your primary point of contact.

At the end of this whole process you will be able to assess whether you can do business with him or her. One point to bear in mind though is that the Manager you are dealing with is unlikely to have the authority to deal with your request. Most banks have centralised all lending decisions or, depending on loan amount even credit scored, so making the concept of 'relationship banking' somewhat difficult to achieve.

If you don't prepare your questions in advance, you may forget about a number of key issues and then you'll have wasted yours and the bank's time by having to go back for another interview.

Step Seven - Rehearse Your Presentation

Great, you've got your sales pitch written out and you've stood for 15 hours in front of your bedroom mirror practising the delivery of all your key points. Sorry. Not good enough!

Every actor will tell you that this is a good short-term technique but it will not do you any favours in the long run; you get used to talking to yourself such that as soon as you move out of the comfort of your bedroom you forget everything you have learnt.

The key is a dress rehearsal with someone taking on the role of the Bank Manager. Going through a mock interview will help you verbalise your answers, something you can't do effectively in front of a mirror, or going through it in your own mind. When rehearsing in front of someone you talk out loud instead of in your mind, where of course the interview has gone perfectly well with the desired result always guaranteed!

Having a live rehearsal will make you realise that all those complicated statements, which sounded great on paper, don't quite sound right when you actually say them.

You need to find someone willing to play the role of the Manager.

They have to understand what you're trying to achieve and, more importantly, take the "interview" seriously if you are going to get the most out of it. As you will do in the real situation, give him a copy of your Business Plan a few days before the mock interview. This will give him time to go through it himself and prepare the questions he would like to ask. This could be the same person you asked to review your Business Plan for accuracy, thereby killing two birds with one stone.

A mock interview is a worthwhile exercise. You may feel embarrassed or think it's a waste of time but it's not; you'll learn a great deal more than you think.

Step Eight - You're Ready To Go!

Arrange Your Appointment

You've rehearsed and practised until you know your Business Plan inside out and now it's time to take the plunge. Ring your bank and ask for an appointment but do not insist on one that afternoon or even the day after. Why? Like all office-based professionals, bankers are people who plan their days in advance. They have business owners to visit and paperwork to follow up on. That cannot be done in a haphazard way with people dropping in at any time, especially those with time consuming requests to borrow money; days need to be planned and you don't want to start on the wrong foot.

Send a Copy of Your Plan

You need to allow your Manager time to read your Plan so you should send a copy as soon as you have confirmed the appointment. This will give him time to review it and to come up with questions to ask or issues to clarify. If you spring a copy of your Plan on him during the interview the session will not be as productive as it could be;

you will simply be called back again or misunderstandings will occur which could be detrimental to the final decision. On this basis it will be easier for him to say no rather than yes, which is not what you want to hear!

When you arrange the appointment tell him you will be sending a copy of the Plan for him to review in advance so at least he will be expecting it.

Prepare a Cover Letter

The manner in which you send the Plan can also help create an impression of professionalism. Here are some tips on writing your cover letter:

- State what the purpose of the meeting is: "to arrange a loan to purchase new business premises", "to arrange an overdraft facility to expand my business".

- Re-confirm the date and time of the meeting. If there has been any mix up on either side it can be put right immediately.

- If you are a start up without any stationery use A4 paper, preferably headed with all your business details. Letterheads can be easily produced on a home computer and will add a touch of professionalism. If you don't have access to a computer then you can get letterheads printed quickly and cheaply at any print shop.

- Make sure the grammar in your covering letter is correct and that there are no spelling mistakes.

- Use the Manager's title and ensure his name is correctly spelt - ring the bank and check if you are not sure.

- The envelope must be new, not a used one! Many business people assume Managers have secretaries to open their mail and that all they will see is the letter itself. This may have been true a few years ago, but not now! The envelope is likely to land on his desk unopened, so this is going to be the first impression he has of you. A used envelope with someone else's address crossed out and a coffee mug stain on it will not create the impression you're looking for! Also, consider the size of the envelope. If you can only just squeeze your Plan into the envelope it's likely to arrive in a sorry state. If it doesn't fit in, buy a bigger envelope!

- As soon as you have spoken to him post the letter via first class mail; you want the proposal to be with him as soon as possible. It will impress him if he gets it the day after your conversation. If you're close enough, you may want to deliver it by hand. However, don't ask to see him in case you are tempted to launch into your presentation; this is neither the time nor the place.

Step Nine - The Day of the Interview

Get Your Appointment Right!

One of the keys to being successful in business is good planning. Ensure all your travel arrangements are in place. If possible make sure you are not dependent on anyone else - Murphy's Law dictates that if something can go wrong, it will go wrong. If you can, rely on no one but yourself.

Next, plan in advance any domestic arrangements such as who is to look after the children or granny! Don't leave all of this to the last minute.

I forget the number of times I waited for business owners to turn up for their appointment only to find out later that they had the wrong time! Don't let this happen to you. Ensure you've got the correct time for the interview. When making the appointment repeat it back to the secretary so there are no misunderstandings on the day of the interview. On the morning of your appointment you may even want to contact the bank to check that the Manager is in. People do go sick and you don't want a wasted journey.

Unforeseen events can happen though and are sufficiently serious that you may not be able to attend the meeting. If this is the case call the bank and either speak to your Manager or leave a message explaining that you can't make it. There is nothing more irritating than sitting around waiting for someone to turn up!

Dress Right!

Having spent time preparing a presentable Business Plan, don't forget that you have to look presentable too. You may think people should never be judged by their appearances, it's what's inside that counts. This is true, but the aim of this book is to give you tips which will give you the edge in getting your proposal agreed. Dressing smartly is one of them. You may disagree that appearances should count but welcome to the real world; people still judge others on their appearances. Don't go to the interview dressed in your favourite jeans, which have been everywhere with you and are considered your best friend!

On the other hand, unless you already run a highly successful business and wearing a suit or a high-powered lady's two-piece is second nature, there is no need to dress as if you're attending a wedding. Some people, who rarely wear general business attire, tend to look uncomfortable when they do, and for some reason this comes across in the way they act.

"The key to any interview situation is to respect the context and the interviewer. You want to appear credible and professional but not so power-dressed that they think

you don't actually need the money. You also want to feel comfortable and relaxed, but not so casual that it veers into scruffy. My advice would be to always dress up one or two notches from your normal comfort zone.

So what does that mean in practical terms? Take a look at the following three statements and decide which best describes you.

I love feeling smart in a suit and think it's the only way to dress for business

Then go ahead and wear your most confidence-boosting suit. However, make sure the suit is not dated, dirty or ill-fitting. Check out the colour and the style – do they both work well for you? If you're not sure, opt for dark navy or dark grey – they're the safest neutrals. Maybe even invest in a personal style consultation.

I don't mind wearing a jacket but wouldn't be seen dead in a tie. I'm creative and contemporary. It's the real me that counts, and not how I dress

Dressing up a notch, in your case, could involve investing in a well-cut jacket or a slightly more expensive blouse, or a shirt which can carry itself without a tie. You may not be wearing black lace up shoes (or courts for women) but the shoe fabric needs to be spotless. Jeans should show no signs of rips, bleaching or frayed hems.

I don't possess a suit, never wear a tie, hate high heels (women only!) and feel happiest in jeans and trainers

If even smart/casual is an alien concept to you, then anything resembling formality will be a challenge but perhaps now is the time to try something new. Ditch the trainers for a pair of casual leather loafers, swap the jeans for a pair of cotton trousers and try a polo shirt rather than the t-shirt. Just making one of these changes adds a little more credibility and reassures the bank manager that you are serious about your business.

One last note about accessories – for both sexes. Keep them minimal and avoid distractions such as "funny" ties/socks/ slogans and excessive bling. Be wary of visible tattoos and facial piercing – your bank manager may not be impressed that you can take that much pain!"

Sue Smart, Positively Smart, www.positivelysmart.com

During interviews I have spent many a time pondering how uncomfortable the customer appears to feel. You don't want to give the Manager a chance for his mind to wander and miss that important point which is crucial to your pitch.

If the only suit or dress you own would not have looked out of place appearing in Saturday Night Fever, then don't wear it! I would spend time marvelling at how well preserved it is and ignoring the wonderfully prepared presentation!

For all the men reading this, do not, under any circumstances, wear the Bart Simpson socks which you were given for Christmas. You may think it creates the impression of a "fun guy", but it's not the image you want to portray! A professional businessman? I don't think so!

Last Minute Check

So now you are set, but before you leave, gather all your papers together, which must include 2 copies of your Business Plan - one for you to refer to and an extra one for the Manager in case he has mislaid the copy you sent in advance! It does and can happen.

Leave in plenty of time. You don't want to be stuck in traffic, get stressed out and be late all at the same time. You have to do everything to make sure you don't throw away all your hard work and blow it within the first few minutes by arriving late, hot and totally stressed.

Those are the nine stages of preparing for the interview. The interview is where it all starts and where it can all finish. Get this wrong and it's all over. Given the interview's importance, re-read the nine steps again and take action on each point.

Don't sit back now and heave a sigh of relief; your preparation doesn't end here. You need to be aware of a few other things which can improve your chances during an interview.

How to Build Rapport

After all your preparations you don't want to spoil it by falling apart during the interview. How you conduct yourself is just as important as the preparation you have put in; some might say even more so. A business owner who comes across as "a good risk" can boost an average Business Plan or idea.

Your aim during the interview is not only to assure the Manager that your business is a bankable proposition but also that you are the type of person he can safely lend money to. Remember, for most small to medium sized businesses the bank is lending to you, not the business.

To achieve the level of comfort the bank is looking for you need to effectively market yourself to get the result you want. Whilst the presentation of your business idea is very important, you are not just selling your business idea, you are selling yourself, your ethics, moral stance, philosophy, skills, and strengths. For a small business, it is these attributes that create or destroy success. Being classed as a 'good risk' is your ultimate goal.

We will see later how important these points are when the bank comes to assess your request but for now bear in mind that everything you do and say in the interview will have a bearing on whether you are assessed as a good or bad risk. Building rapport between you and the Manager is part of this process.

Let's look at some of the tools and strategies you can use to build rapport to achieve a win/win outcome.

Speak With Confidence

There's no getting away from it, human nature is such that we naturally feel more comfortable with people who are confident and can express their ideas and thoughts with conviction. Your voice has to convey your inner strength. It has to say to the listener, "I'm going to make a success of this business" or "I know that the additional money I'm asking for will help me increase turnover by 100%".

Your voice is an expression of the strong belief you have in yourself. This links back to the first of the 9 steps in preparing for an interview - having belief. You can believe what you want but unless your voice conveys that strength of belief then convincing another party that you are worthy of support will be hard. People are drawn to those who are confident. Portraying confidence will help create rapport.

A much-quoted study about communication, carried out by Professor Albert Mehrabian, analysed the process of how we get ideas and thoughts across to others. He said:

- 55% of communication is carried through body language
- 38% through the tone of voice
- 7% through the actual words we use

The study findings (often abbreviated to the '3 Vs' – visual, vocal, verbal) indicate that an amazing 93% of our communication style has absolutely nothing to do with the words we use. The conclusion to draw from these findings is that you can use as many words as you like on how your business is going to expand, how successful it's going to be and how you have the skills to make it all happen, but these will only count for 7% of the message; 38% of your message is conveyed in your tone of voice. Imagine that!

So how can you positively influence the tone of your voice?

Sound Confident

The learning point from Mehrabian's study is that you have to *sound* confident - don't speak too quietly. A softly spoken person is assumed, rightly or wrongly, to be timid in nature and timid people tend not to come across as dynamic business owners! The Manager will think, "How is this person going to sell their products to customers if he can't even sell me the initial idea of what his business is about?"

On the other hand, don't speak too loudly either. People who speak too loudly come across as over-bearing, over-confident, and too "full of themselves". Think of the number of people you've come across like this. What was your immediate impression? "I don't like him!" That's not what you want your Manager to say!

Remember, as a small business he is lending to you as an individual; the business is secondary. You have to convince him that *you* are worthy of support. The bottom line is that you have to make him connect with you.

The difficult bit is to strike a balance between being too quiet and too loud. You need to get to the point where your tone of voice says, "I know what I'm doing. I can make a success of this."

If you don't know at which end of the scale you are, ask someone whom you trust for his or her honest opinion and then act upon their comments. Listen to what they say and make a conscious effort to change your style.

Don't Sound Boring!

As well as your voice sound level you have to ensure your voice portrays enthusiasm and this is achieved through your tonality. You have to sound enthusiastic. How many people have you met and within 2 minutes you are desperately trying to stifle a yawn? The content of what they are saying may be of interest and the conviction in their voice may make you believe in what they're saying but they speak in one long monotonous tone. It's so boring!

To convey enthusiasm, vary your tonality and emphasise certain words (especially success-based words, which we will discuss later). All of this will make it much more interesting for the listener and so keep him wanting to listen.

Listen to How Others Do It

Start listening to how other people speak. If you have confidence or belief in a certain person, analyse how they speak, what gives you that feeling of confidence? What is it they do to make you feel that way? On the other hand, if you come across someone whom you don't feel comfortable with, again ask yourself why. How does he speak and use his voice? What exactly pushes you away from him? Why don't you feel comfortable?

By making an effort to listen you'll soon pick up the good and bad points of how others communicate. Learn from it and put it into practice. If you have a problem with sounding confident during your mock interview specifically ask your role-playing Bank Manager to focus in on this issue. Hone your new skills on your family and friends so that when you come to the big day it's second nature.

Your Body Language Can Speak Volumes!

Another way to help build rapport is to understand the importance of body language. During our caveman years we communicated via grunts and gestures. Body language played a central part of the communication process and that has stayed with us - so ignore it at your peril!

Professor Mehrabian's study indicated that 55% of the communication process is carried through body language. When putting across a case to borrow money, your Bank Manager is going to be influenced, either positively or negatively, by your body language.

To make sure you give out only positive vibes consider these aspects of your body language.

Make Plenty of Eye Contact

Stare him straight in the eyes when you want to put across a particularly powerful point; this demonstrates confidence. Avoiding eye contact gives the impression you are so uncomfortable with what you're saying that you can't look him in the eye. Your discomfort could give the Manager the feeling that you either lack confidence or are lying.

Not looking him in the eye, especially during crucial statements, will lead to him thinking, "He's trying to hide something. What is it?" or "He doesn't seem very comfortable with what he just said. Has he got a problem in that area?"

I once interviewed someone who barely looked at me; he spent the majority of the interview with his eyes fixed to my desk! It was so noticeable that I hardly listened to what he was saying. The question of what he had to hide, why he was so lacking in confidence, was constantly going through my mind.

I think you can guess that he never got his overdraft! He just didn't convince me that he could make a success of being in business. Your eyes can give away so much about your thoughts. Make sure they say you are confident, not afraid of the task ahead and worthy of support.

Watch Your Posture

Your posture can also say a lot about you. Sit up straight, don't slouch in the chair (I know, I sound like your mother but it's true!) Spreading yourself across the chair gives the impression you don't care about how you look, that you don't pay attention to detail. It can also give the impression you don't really want to be there and projects an attitude that says, "I'm better than you. Why do I have to come here and beg for money? Give me my loan and let me get on with it."

Someone sitting up straight says that this person is ready for action, enthusiastic and ready to take on the world!

Smile!

A miserable person is not going to endear themselves to anyone. It's a fact that we gravitate to people who are happy and smiling. They appear to be having a ball in life and we want to be part of it! If you walked into a department store and you had the choice of two assistants, one who was smiling and welcoming and one who was down-in-the-mouth, who would you choose to go to?

A smile has the power to melt away any opposition or ill feeling. It's another aspect of our body language, which shouts out confidence and helps build rapport.

Watch His Body Language

You will be able to gauge your Manager's initial reactions by observing his body language and reacting to that. If you learn to read body language in other people then misunderstandings can be rectified early on and you'll get an important insight into what the other person is thinking.

Here are some of the things to look out for:

- If you see him leaning back in his chair, it's almost as if he's trying to get as far away from you as possible. The hidden meaning could be that he's trying to distance himself from what you are proposing; in other words he doesn't like your idea. If you see this, you need to immediately find out what is on his mind, so ask a question. Ask if he has any comments on what you've said so far and this will give you the chance to get him back on side. If he has misunderstood something which has led him to switching off, then it's important you clarify the problem, correct it and move on.

- If he has started supporting his head with his hands under his chin, it may be that he has lost interest in what you're saying. If you see this "loss-of-interest" signal, again ask a question such as "Do you have any queries so far?" Asking questions of someone who looks bored or left out brings them back into the conversation and again gives you an opportunity to check their understanding of what you have covered.

- The opposite of the "bored pose", is where he starts leaning towards you. This may indicate a high level of interest in what you have to say and shows that you're on the right track. Spotting this will help improve your confidence even further.

- Crossed arms and legs may indicate a negative feeling

towards your proposal. Again, ask questions to uncover what the problem or concern is, so you can clear up any misunderstandings.

- If he is maintaining a very "open" position i.e. arms apart, nodding in agreement, he is indicating that he's keen to know more about your project and so giving you the green light to carry on with your presentation.

As I mentioned, if you do see evidence of negative body language, ask questions to get him to express his feelings or thoughts. Such questions would be: "What do you think about what I've covered so far?", "From what you've heard so far, what are your impressions?" or "Have I made myself clear?"

The last question is a closed question - a question to which there is only a yes or no answer. Such a question is still useful to establish understanding; listen to the answer for the tonality and watch his body language. If a yes answer is given, implying he understands, but the tone is hesitant and the way he shuffles in his seat implies discomfort, then you'll know he doesn't really understand and this is your cue to go over some of the key points again.

Having a basic grasp of body language and its hidden meanings can help you gain the edge during an interview. Spend time researching the subject and you will be justly rewarded.

Learn To Use Success-Based Words

You will recall that Albert Mehrabian said words account for only 7% of the communication process. It may not sound a lot yet this 7% could be the difference between success and failure. Words are powerful enough to start and stop wars or convey love and hate, so it's important that we use the right words when we do communicate.

We all take words for granted. We are taught a basic vocabulary in school and then build on that during the rest of our lifetime as we grow and learn. It's estimated that there are in excess of three million words in the English language but we use only a small percentage. Estimates are that individually we only use 1/2 percent to 2 percent of the words available to us. Invariably we use the words which everyone else in our social group or background uses.

As a successful or potentially successful business person, you do not want to be using the same dull words as the general masses. In line with your strong belief and confident talking style, you need to use words which propel you above the average person and reinforce the belief you have in your success.

Your words have to shout out that here is a successful person who knows what he wants! The words you use have to convey your enthusiasm and energy - all of which is necessary to run a successful business. Changing your vocabulary to a "success-based" one will take some practice and constant vigilance on your part. So what substituted success-based words should you be using in your conversation?

Try and think of the words you use on a daily basis. Do they convey what you really want to say? Are they non success-based or success-based? Can you change them to ones that are?

ORDINARY WORD	SUCCESS-BASED WORD
alright	superb
ready	raring to go
enthusiastic	excited
good	phenomenal
interested	captivated
fine	fantastic
O.K	couldn't be better

Success-based words are the ideal ones to emphasise. Properly emphasised words can further convey power, success, confidence and a strong belief.

Filler Words and Phrases

Whilst on the use of words, be careful of littering your conversation with "filler" words or phrases. These are words or phrases which serve no purpose and add nothing to your message; they are actually a distraction for the listener. Examples of such fillers are: "Um", "you know what I mean"; "ahhh..."; "kinda like".

These fillers dilute your message and imply that you're not a decisive person. Make a conscious effort not to punctuate your presentation with these fillers. You can achieve this by preparing your script containing your key points and rehearsing it. Knowing your script means your brain doesn't have the chance to pause, slip into neutral and then go to sleep!

So watch the words you use. Use words and phrases that have passion and send out a clear message that you are ready to take on the world and make a success of your business.

After The Preparation ... The Interview!

If you gave the Manager plenty of time to read your Business Plan before the agreed meeting date and you have heard nothing from him, you can safely assume that he is sufficiently interested in your proposal to continue with the meeting as planned.

So, there you are, sitting outside his office waiting to be summoned. You have prepared as much as you can and now is the time to put it all into action. What can you expect? How can you put all that you have learnt into action?

In this section we are going to look at how to handle yourself during the interview.

The Waiting Game

In days gone by, senior people often played the power game of making you wait before being called in, just to show who was boss! Banking was no different. However I think I'm safe in saying that those days are gone. If you do end up having to wait, it will be for a genuine reason, so don't get wound up! Use it as an opportunity to relax and mentally prepare.

The Introduction

If it's the first time you have met, firmly shake your Manager's hand, look her in the eye, smile and confidently introduce yourself. The first minute or so is usually reserved for breaking the ice, asking if the journey was OK, whether you had trouble parking. Use this opportunity to settle yourself down and get comfortable.

Your Opening

Here's where you now unleash your killer opening statement which we discussed earlier! It could be, for example, "Thank you for seeing me today. I trust you have had the chance to review my Business Plan. As you know, I am looking for a loan to ......"

Whatever it is, remember that first impressions count, so confidently start the interview with a strong opening line.

You're Off

Once you have finished your opening statement, the interview is on. You can expect the meeting to last anything from 30 minutes to an hour, depending on the complexity of your business and your request. The Manager will be asking the majority of questions (most of which you will have anticipated, of course!) and, if the interview is handled correctly, you will be doing the majority of the talking. Remember to put into action, or be aware of, everything we covered earlier:

- Speaking with confidence
- Watching both your and her body language and asking questions if she looks bored or doesn't understand
- Using success-based words
- Being open and honest about you and your business
- And generally building rapport, establishing your credibility, integrity and honesty

Don't Bluff

No matter how well prepared you are, she will no doubt come up with questions to which you don't know the answers. Don't bluff your way through; if you're not sure, tell her you'll get back to her. There is nothing worse than someone coming up with an answer that is plainly rubbish. Don't believe that the Manager won't pick up on a top-of-the-head answer. Your voice, conviction and general body language will say it all ... you don't know the answer so you made it up or guessed. Don't bluff.

Just the Facts!

When talking about your business and your future plans it is easy to become very emotional about the whole thing. Yes, it is good to show that you care about your business but if the purpose of the meeting with the bank is to ask for a top up to your existing loan or overdraft in order to keep the business going, then don't go overboard. Don't go down on bended knees and beg! Just stick to the facts and let your Business Plan do the talking.

Taking Notes

Bring a notebook with you and use it to jot down any issues or questions you need to get back to her on. The notebook is also useful for you to have a record of her answers to the queries or questions you put to her. A notebook and pen in hand sends out a very clear signal as to your efficiency and seriousness in doing business.

Ask Your Questions

Don't forget to ask all those questions you have prepared. Not asking any questions is the style of an unseasoned business person. Savvy business people want to know all the ins and outs and so must you. You must be inquiring, and inquisitive.

Bear in mind that your questions should not give the impression that you want your money at any cost. You have to be interested in the terms and conditions on offer, such as the interest rate to be charged, any other costs and the security you will be expected to provide.

Negotiate Interest Rates and Charges Now

Whilst it may be tempting to wait until you get an offer to talk about interest rates and charges, do it now. It's better to have this conversation early on in the discussion so you know where you stand. It's unlikely the Manager will have the last say on charges, especially when he has to seek approval for your facility from a higher authority, but at least you will have a ballpark figure to play with.

No doubt you have negotiated with many suppliers and a bank is no different, and yet the tide has turned against business owners over the last few years when it comes to negotiating a good deal. The last two to three years has seen the availability of funds and the willingness of banks to lend money rapidly decline. In the 'boom' years the power in any negotiation was invariably with the business owner – competition amongst banks was such that they were afraid to lose any business so could be flexible on rates and charges.

The position though changed within a matter of months and any leverage in the negotiation was then firmly with the banks. With competition almost non-existent and finance being tough to get the answer you were likely to get is, "This is the price. That's it." After all, where are you to go? The high cost of borrowing has been a bugbear with small businesses and sometimes has created a very high cost barrier which has been difficult to climb.

This will change though. Competition will eventually return and banks will again be hungry for business. So practise your negotiation skills and be bold enough to tackle the cost now, don't wait for the market to change!

Points to Consider When Negotiating

Set Your Objectives – decide what interest rate and fees you are prepared to pay. At what point would you walk away?

Preparation – know your strengths and weaknesses; know your bargaining points and what you are prepared to give away for a better interest rate.

Brush Up on Your Listening Skills – listen for the real meaning of what the Manager is saying. Are there hidden clues that the cost can be reduced if you push enough?

Be Flexible – don't play the 'hard man' and throw away a deal because you are stubbornly sticking to what you want; read the signs, listen to the other side of the argument and be prepared to provide concessions if necessary.

Build a Relationship - your aim is to maintain and build a lasting relationship; backing your Manager into a corner is going to build a strong relationship. Aim for a win/win – you win, he wins.

Make Him Tout For Your Business!

The Manager will have targets for new business so it's important for you to realise that he needs you just as much as you need him. Recently, given past events, banks' appetite for new business has reduced but this will reverse over time and competition in the market will return.

To get the bank working hard to win your business ask questions such as,

- "I've been around a few banks; why should I bank with you?"
- "What will you do for my business?"
- "If I have a problem, how will you handle my request for help?"
- "When you're away on holiday, who can I refer to if I need help or advice?"

Make her sweat for your business; this is not a one-way street! Tackling her on these issues demonstrates that you can be a hard-nosed business person who wants the best from all your deals. Her answers will also give you the chance to gauge whether you can work with her.

You have to feel happy with your choice of Manager; he or she is the one you are going to be working closely with. You have to feel comfortable in ringing her up and asking for help or advice. If you think it's going to be difficult establishing a rapport, then move on and find someone else.

The Closing

In winding up the meeting you should use your pre-prepared closing statement, which we discussed earlier. It should encapsulate everything you have said and be a positive close to the meeting, leaving the Manager with the feeling that you are the type of person the bank can do business with.

As with any meeting, before you leave you should ask what the next step is, what action will be taken and when you can expect to hear from them.

The meeting can end in one of three ways:

- Your Plan may not have contained all the information the Manager was looking for. If so, he will ask you to go and gather all the additional information he needs and then request you to arrange a further appointment.

- He will give you his decision on the spot – 'no'. An immediate 'no' at the end of the meeting is a very clear signal that your request is one she can't support and it's better not to waste any more time!

- An immediate 'yes' answer is unlikely because she will probably want time to consider the information gleaned from you during the meeting. She will also have to go through the formal analysis of your request and then submit the proposal to a higher level for review and approval. So the 3rd and most likely outcome of your meeting is that she says she'll come back to you within a certain timescale. Make sure she has all your contact details or that she knows they are contained in your Business Plan.

Leaving the Meeting

When leaving, pick up all your things, shake her hand and with confidence look her in the eyes and say goodbye.

What Happens Next?

After you have left the bank premises you must be thinking, "I've spent hours and days working on that Business Plan and all they did was ask me questions on things already included in it! I bet they'll hardly look at that Plan. It'll probably end up in the bin."

If there is a deal to be done nothing could be further from the truth. Your Business Plan is going to be used as the basis for the evaluation of your proposal. Without that mammoth overview of your project she would have to summarise the information that came out of the interview and you could only hope that she captured the essence of what you were trying to put across. Your Business Plan has done this for you.

So what exactly happens after you leave the bank? How will your Manager assess your request? What is the process? Is there one?

By the end of the next few chapters you will understand the bank's thinking and this will further help you get the correct information submitted at the very start of the process. To provide you with an insight into the banker's world we will be looking at each of the areas the bank considers and examining the framework used to assess your request. We will start with your Financial Statements.

READING AND UNDERSTANDING YOUR FINANCIAL STATEMENTS

In this chapter we will start our look at how the bank analyses your Financial Statements and what they can tell about your business. This will not only give you an understanding of what the bank looks for in your figures but it also gives you the tools to help you assess your own performance. By the end of this chapter you'll know exactly what your accountant and Bank Manager is talking about!

You may find this heavy going. Looking at facts and figures is not everyone's idea of heaven, but stick with me. It's essential that you have a grasp of the numbers side of your business. You may think that your service, the products you provide and dealing with suppliers is the nub of your business but without an understanding of the numbers you are not completing the picture.

So, let's agree that you'll read the next few chapters and not skip ahead!

Financial Statements

What Are Financial Statements?

One of the first things your Manager will review after your interview will be your performance, as reflected in your Financial Statements. For those of you who are just starting out in business, or if you've not really taken any interest in accounts, what are they exactly?

Financial Statements are annual statements drawn up by an accountant (or yourself if you are sufficiently proficient), which detail your financial performance and financial position as at the date the accounts were drawn. The Statements feature two sets of figures: Profit and Loss Account and Balance Sheet.

Profit And Loss Account

The Profit and Loss account, referred to as the P & L, will show:

- Sales
- Cost of raw materials or stock
- Overheads
- Profit or loss

Balance Sheet

The Balance Sheet will show:

- Fixed assets (land and machinery etc)
- Current assets (stock, debtors and cash)
- Liabilities (creditors, overdrafts and loans)
- Capital invested or held in the business
- The worth of the business

Financial Statements are a year-by-year overview of how your business has performed and they can show a lot about the strength, or otherwise, of a business. Accounts are also useful to compare key areas of how a business is doing against other businesses in the same industry. For example, businesses in the same sector should, within reason, be producing comparable gross profit margins and have similar terms of trade. If the business being assessed is out of line with the rest of the industry then this begs the question as to why. What are you doing differently?

Obviously if your business is a start up, no Accounts will be available, so the Manager will pay attention to the financial projections or forecasts contained in your Business Plan. For an established business, a review of your past performance can say a lot about future ability to pay and any potential problems.

Why It Pays To Keep Your Financial Statements Up To Date

Analysis of the Accounts forms an important part of the bank's assessment process and so it's important to keep your figures and records up to date. Imagine if you are slow in submitting your figures to your accountant, suddenly a good business opportunity comes up which you can't afford to miss but you don't have all the cash available, so you have to run to the bank.

On approaching your bank for support, the first thing they ask for are your Accounts, which of course you don't have! You put pressure on your accountant to finish the books as quickly as possible but the superb opportunity slips away because the bank can't get an answer to you quickly enough. The key reason the bank could not react quickly is that you just didn't have all the information immediately to hand.

I have seen many businesses which unexpectedly need an overdraft or loan facility, and yet don't have up to date figures, and so either the opportunity is missed or the whole process of assessment and review takes weeks.

You never know when you will need assistance from the bank and by their very nature opportunities are always unexpected. So keep on top of your books.

Knowledge Can Be Useful

The majority of business owners will admit that when it comes to their Financial Statements a mist falls over their eyes! The figures, which the accountant diligently produces each year, mean absolutely nothing to them. With even a basic understanding of what to look for, an examination of your Accounts can better help you understand your business and assist you in making decisions about what changes to make. You will be able to better understand the cycles within your business and at least be aware of any potential pitfalls. Knowledge such as this could help you avoid making costly mistakes.

Figures in isolation mean very little. The key behind analysing a set of Accounts is to ask questions:

- "Why is that figure getting worse each year?"
- "Why am I only making that much profit?"
- "What would happen if I collected money owed to me quicker?"

These are only some of the questions an understanding of Accounts can prompt. Knowledge of how to analyse will help you get behind the figures and understand what they really mean.

You may read the following pages and think you don't need to know all this. Well, you may be right, but you will recall earlier we said it was important during the interview stage for you to know your figures. Knowing by repeating parrot fashion a string of numbers is not the same as having in depth knowledge and understanding. Make every effort to read and digest the following sections so you'll be better prepared for the questions your Manager will ask.

Limitations of Accounts

Before we look at the techniques used to analyse Accounts, you have to realise that, despite me saying how essential they are, Financial Statements do have their limitations:

- They are a snapshot of the business as at the day they are drawn up. They reveal very little about the ups and downs during the year or how the business looked on any other day of the financial year.

- Although an accountant prepares the annual accounts he is very much relying on the business owner to provide all the necessary and correct information. If the owner decides not to declare a percentage of sales which were transacted in cash or decides to hold invoices over to the next year to reduce profits, there is little the accountant can do about it. Don't expect the bank to be too sympathetic if your "Inland Revenue prepared" figures don't justify bank support - the phrase "you can't have your cake and eat it" springs to mind!

- Accounts look back at historic, not future, events. They show what the business did in sales and profit but that doesn't mean that this will be replicated in future years.

- The figures reveal nothing about management style, the trading environment the business operates in, or the quality of its workforce. The figures are rather dry and it's difficult to bring the business to life.

- By the time the business owner has done the preparation and the accountant has produced the Accounts, it can take up to 6 months before they are available (sometimes more). Accounts are therefore stale by the time they are finalised - a major weakness if used as a standalone assessment tool.

- The other problem caused by extensive delays is that it is possible for a business not to realise it is loss making for up to 12 months after the losses started to occur. For example, XYZ Ltd starts its new financial year on 1st January and for 6 months it trades profitability. However, from 1st July it starts making losses. Let's say it takes 6 months after the year-end to produce the Accounts and so the change in profitability is not picked up until July the following year, one year after losses started occurring. This assumes that a liquidity crisis hasn't hit during that time to highlight the problem and that the year's profit is lower than that of the previous years, thereby prompting questions. If you have a superb first six months this could further mask the dramatic change in performance.

- This example not only shows the importance of getting Financial Statements prepared as quickly as possible but also the benefit of having regular financial information produced on a monthly or quarterly basis. By producing regular figures any shift in profitability can be spotted very early on and action taken.

Management Accounts

We have seen that Annual Accounts have a number of disadvantages as a tool for monitoring the performance of a business. Obtaining management accounts can overcome some of these weaknesses. Management figures are essentially annual accounts drawn up on a weekly, monthly or quarterly basis. Many smaller firms do not have the luxury of employing in-house accountants, so the format can be very simple, but there are a number of PC-based packages which make the task of putting figures together very much easier and help in interpretation.

"What if things are going wrong in your business and you don't know it? You can't fix the problem early and before you know it, the problem has "stolen" money right out of your wallet.

It works the same way with opportunities too... miss one because you don't have your performance measures in place and you are making your business life much harder than it needs to be.

In my opinion, understanding how your business is performing, and especially the few key drivers of profit and cash flow, is essential for anyone who wants to manage for profit and not leave it to luck."

Paul Simister, Your Profit Coach,
www.yourprofitcoach.co.uk

A business of any size should have no excuse not to produce regular financial information. If you don't know how you are performing how do you know what problems, if any, need to be put right? A dip in sales, a fall in margins or a sudden undetected increase in costs can be spotted very quickly if management accounts are produced.

The Four Key Areas of Assessment

The Manager doesn't just pick up the Accounts to see if a profit has been made and then casually put them back in the file. Financial Statements can reveal a lot about a firm's strengths and weaknesses.

Within the assessment process there are four key areas to focus on, each of which have ratios that can be calculated and reviewed to provide an overview of business performance.

The four areas are:

- The *Net Worth* of the business and the relationship between the money you have invested in the business and funds you have borrowed
- The *liquidity* of the business which assesses your ability to meet day-to-day debts or commitments as they fall due
- *Profitability*, which I hope is self explanatory!
- *Serviceability* which is the business' ability to repay its debts or cover its interest payments

Even though an assessment can be made from just one year's Accounts, a fairer reflection is obtained by comparing a minimum of two years' figures but ideally three years. By doing this, you can spot trends, and trends are more revealing than figures read in isolation. As we will see, reviewing the trends from year to year is the basis of an assessment of your trading performance and financial strength.

In the next few chapters we are going to look at a fictitious company's Annual Accounts and examine the assessment process so you can understand what bankers are looking for. Not only will this help you to better manage your finances but you will be able to speak the same language as your Manager and so have more meaningful business review sessions.

BALANCE SHEET ASSESSMENT – WHAT'S YOUR BUSINESS WORTH?

In order to demonstrate how an assessment is built up and what is regarded as a strength or weakness, let's assume the bank has received a request from XYZ Ltd for a loan and they have handed in their Profit and Loss and Balance Sheet.

In this chapter we will look at the Balance Sheet and examine the key points which banks are most interested in.

Net Worth Assessment

The Net Worth, or Net Tangible Assets as it is sometimes referred to, is what the business is worth if it was sold on the day the Balance Sheet was compiled, and the asset and liability figures quoted were the amounts actually paid or realised.

Net Worth is calculated by taking all the assets and deducting all the liabilities; what's left is the worth of the business – the Net Worth. Obviously to achieve the Net Worth figure detailed in the Accounts, you would have to sell all assets and pay off all the liabilities at the exact figures quoted in the Balance Sheet, something that is unlikely to happen.

BALANCE SHEET FOR XYZ LTD
31ST DECEMBER 20X1 AND 20X2

	20X1		20X2	
FIXED ASSETS				
Land, Equipment		200,500		211,200
CURRENT ASSETS				
Stock	56,700		53,400	
Debtors	15,600		21,300	
Cash in Hand	1,300		1,050	
	73,600		75,750	
CURRENT LIABILITIES				
Bank Overdraft	10,400		14,500	
Creditors	30,900		22,400	
	41,300		36,900	
NET CURRENT ASSETS		32,300		38,850
Long Term Loan		-48,700		-45,550
NET WORTH		184,100		204,500
FUNDED BY				
Share Capital		100,000		100,000
Retained Profit		84,100		104,500
NET WORTH		184,100		204,500

For companies that have an investment in 'hard assets' such as property, plant and machinery, then the Net Worth figure is a reasonably tangible amount and provides a guideline as to what the business could be worth if broken up on the day the Accounts were drawn. This is more difficult for service related businesses or businesses that operate in the virtual world. The worth of the business is intangible and can only be truly established when it comes to working out the goodwill factor; what value can you put on a brand or goodwill?

Let's look at XYZ's Net Worth. As at the end of December 20X1, if XYZ Ltd decided to close down and the fixed assets were sold and realised £200,500, the current assets realised £73,600, then with current liabilities of £41,300 and a bank loan of £48,700 to be paid off, the figure left would be £184,100. This is XYZ's Net Worth.

There are two questions the bank will ask about a business' Net Worth.

Is The Business Solvent?

The first test is to see if the business is solvent. This means, do the company's assets exceed its liabilities? If so, then the business is solvent but if liabilities exceed assets then it's insolvent. In XYZ Ltd's case in 20X1, it is solvent, to the tune of £184,100.

There are a number of businesses which do have insolvent Balance Sheets because of past problems, mainly due to accumulated losses. They can survive if carefully managed and are moving back into profit, thereby reducing the deficit. If a business is insolvent, it's not a reason to close down but it is a warning sign that, during a period of sustained crisis or loss making, the business may have problems in surviving. Limited Company directors need to take professional advice if the business appears to be insolvent. Trading under such circumstances can lead to problems if the business ultimately closes.

The issue of solvency is important when it comes to considering the day-to-day liquidity of the business i.e. its ability to meet debts as and when they fall due. We will be looking at this aspect of solvency later on.

The Net Worth of a business can be compared to fat reserves which animals carry; during winter, or periods when there is little food around, animals live off their reserves. This survival technique applies to a company which suffers a lean period; its Net Worth is its fat reserve, which it uses to carry it through to better times. If it doesn't have a reserve, or a very poor one, then a long spell of losses can be hard to ride out and could lead to closure.

Is The Net Worth Growing?

The next thing the Manager will look at is whether the Net Worth of the business is growing or a deficit reducing. If it is heading in a positive direction, then this indicates that profits are being retained within the business and so the financial structure of the business is getting stronger.

XYZ Ltd has seen its Net Worth grow by £20,400, which is represented by the amount of profit retained in the year-end 20X2. So, for XYZ Ltd, this is a good start to the assessment, and the Manager would assess the Net Worth as a strength.

The Net Worth of a business could grow through means other than retained profits. An injection of capital or fresh cash by the directors will improve the financial health of the business. In XYZ's case, if the directors had increased capital by a further £10,000 then in 20X2, their Net Worth would be £214,500.

If the Net Worth has been declining then this can be attributed to two outcomes or a combination of both: losses or withdrawal of capital. A fall in Net Worth is seen as a weakness because the business' reserves have been depleted, thereby increasing the risk of the business not being able to withstand a shock, either internal or external.

The ideal situation is where a business' Net Worth grows year-by-year through retained profits.

Gearing

Gearing is the ratio of borrowed money within the business compared to its Net Worth. A business is considered to be highly geared when borrowed money in relation to its Net Worth is high. A low-geared business is where borrowed money is low in relation to Net Worth.

Gearing is worked out as follows:

borrowed money (overdrafts and loans) less cash held
Net Worth

The major problem with being highly geared is that the business is vulnerable to higher interest charges or pressing creditors and so the inherent risk within the business is higher.

There is no ideal ratio because it really depends on which industry the business is in. The standard measure of whether a company is considered to be highly geared though is a ratio of greater than 1:1. The test as to whether carrying a high gearing is a risk is the business' ability to generate cash to meet day-to-day demands for payment. For example, a business which is selling goods very rapidly can afford to be highly geared because they are realising cash very quickly (assuming favourable terms of trade) and so they could satisfy any immediate demand, within reason, for cash from creditors. On the other hand, a highly geared firm which only turns over stock, for example, every 2 months, may find it difficult to meet an immediate cash demand.

It's all about having strong cash flows and the ability of the business to service its debts as and when they fall due. Which category are you in?

Correctly structuring your company's borrowing by having some on overdraft, some on loan or a mixture of the two is important. Too much on overdraft puts the business at the mercy of the bank because they can demand immediate repayment, whereas if the majority of the borrowing is on loan, then the business is protected in that as long the repayments are kept up to date, the debt cannot be "called in". We will look at this in more depth later.

Being correctly structured is about having long term assets financed on loan, not overdraft. It's back to having the liquidity to meet debts as they fall due.

Having a poor gearing is not a recipe for disaster, it just needs to be watched and the implications understood.

XYZ's gearing is:

20X1:   57,800 / 184,100   =   0.31

20X2:   59,000 / 204,500   =   0.29

In this case, XYZ's dependence on borrowed money has reduced during the 2 years. Even though their net borrowing actually increased by £1,200, the ratio improved because their Net Worth increased due to retained profits. In assessing XYZ's gearing, the bank would class this as a strength.

If gearing had increased, then the Manager will look at the accounts to see where the problem lies. It could be because losses were made, thereby reducing Net Worth, or more money could have been borrowed, or a combination of both.

Gearing is a useful ratio to assess a business' ability to meet a sudden cash demand.

Liquidity Assessment

The next area to assess is the liquidity position of the business. When reviewing gearing I said that a company can be highly geared and yet not be a risk, because it can turn assets such as stock and debtors into cash very quickly. The quicker they can do this then the better their ability to meet sudden cash demands. This position describes a liquid business; an illiquid business is one where stock and debtors are slow moving and so there is limited ability to immediately settle a call by creditors.

Liquidity is worked out as follows:

current assets less current liabilities = net current assets

Current assets are defined as assets which can be turned into cash immediately or relatively quickly. Such assets include cash, debtors, and stock (assuming the latter is a fast-turnover item).

Current liabilities are defined as liabilities which can be demanded for repayment immediately. Such liabilities include all creditors and bank overdrafts.

If current assets exceed current liabilities then the business is liquid, but if current liabilities are greater than current assets then the business is illiquid.

Let's consider XYZ's liquidity position.

You can see from the Balance Sheet that in 20X2 the company had Net Current Assets totalling £38,850. This figure has been arrived at by taking current assets and deducting current liabilities, which in this case leaves a surplus of £38,850. So XYZ Ltd is liquid to the tune of £38,850. In other words, if all of XYZ's creditors, totalling £22,400 in 20X2, demanded payment in one go, then on the face of it XYZ would be able to pay up.

However, by saying the business is liquid, we are assuming that all, or some of, the stock is readily saleable and that all debtors can be collected quickly in order to meet a demand. If a business has stock which traditionally takes time to move, or debtors which are on long credit terms, then because of the mix within each asset class the business may not be as fully liquid as the figures suggest.

The only way for the bank to find out is by asking questions about the make up of the debtor book and stock. So just looking at the current assets figure on its own is not enough; you have to ask how quickly your current assets can be turned into cash to assess how liquid you are.

Remember, the key to analysing accounts is all about asking the right questions to uncover the real position - the figures on their own may not reveal everything you need to know about your business.

However, the basic question is whether the business can convert assets into cash within a reasonable timescale to meet immediate and unexpected payment demands i.e. is the business liquid? On the face of it XYZ is.

The Working Capital Cycle and the Importance of Cash

The difference between current assets and current liabilities, as well as being known as net current assets, is also generally termed as working capital. Working capital is the oxygen or life blood of any business - it keeps the business going on a day-to-day basis. No working capital, no business.

The continuing success of a business is down to its ability to continue recycling debtors and stock into cash so it can again be reinvested into more stock or payment of creditors, leading to more sales and eventually turning back into debtors or cash. Executed correctly, the cycle should be flawless and never-ending. This is known as the working capital cycle.

In some instances businesses can't turn debtors and finished stock into cash quick enough to meet their demands for more raw materials, stock or repayment of creditors. This may be down to the fact that to be competitive the business is forced to give extended payment terms to its customers. As a result, because cash is tied up in debtors for longer, without outside help the business would have to stop production of new goods or buying more stock until cash is released from debtors, so allowing the cycle to start again. You would then have a business which is constantly in "stop-start" mode. Not an effective way to run a business!

If the working capital cycle is not turning over in an even manner it can be difficult for a business to substantially increase sales without outside help or support. This is where bank overdrafts and creditors, who provide stock and raw materials on credit terms, come in; they effectively "bridge" the gap between money being made available and money being needed to continue production.

The cycle, supported by the bank or creditors, works as follows:

-   An overdraft limit would allow you to buy goods immediately and it's paid back once debtors pay up, or
-   Suppliers that provide goods or raw materials on credit means you can take the product now, sell it and settle up once cash is released by debtors.

Some businesses can depend solely on creditors to bridge any working capital gap. For example, if you can buy stock and raw materials on 90 days' credit and then on-sell giving 30 days' credit, you will be cash positive because you get your money in before you have to pay it back i.e. you get cash from sales in 30 days but don't have to pay suppliers for another 60 days.

If your terms of trade are the other way round, with suppliers only giving you 30 days and debtors taking 90 days to pay you, then your business is cash negative. In this instance you would have to rely on an overdraft to help finance the gap if you or the business didn't have sufficient cash reserves.

A working capital cycle looks like the diagram shown below.

The cycle starts with having cash, an overdraft or creditors willing to give credit terms. These funds are used to purchase stock or raw materials, which are then transformed into work in progress. Once completed they are stored as finished goods, sold and eventually converted into debtors. After the period of credit (if any) debtors pay up and are converted into cash and so the cycle starts again with either the cash being used to reduce the overdraft, pay off creditors or utilised to finance the continuation of the cycle.

WORKING CAPITAL CYCLE

CASH, OVERDRAFT OR CREDITORS

▼

STOCK/RAW MATERIALS

▼

WORK IN PROGRESS

▼

FINISHED GOODS

▼

DEBTORS

This model assumes that the cycle is completely sealed and continues uninterrupted in that no other cash comes in or out of the business but we know of course that this is not true. The working capital cycle or cash flow can be affected, negatively or positively, by these injections and drains.

INJECTIONS	DRAINS
Cash Injection	Cash Withdrawal
Sale Of Fixed Assets	Purchases Of Fixed Assets
New or Additional Bank Loans	Repayment Of Bank Loans
Profits	Dividends
	Overheads
	Losses

The effect of a drain in cash, or withdrawal of cash, means that cash is no longer available within the cycle to buy stock or finance work-in-progress pending debtors being collected. A large enough cash drain or withdrawal on a regular basis, or the purchase of a large capital item, can cause the cycle to stall. You can see why purchasing a capital item out of cash flow is not a good idea – it sucks cash out of the working capital cycle. Purchases such as this need to be funded via a loan, not cash, unless you have a large enough reserve to cope with a large outflow.

On the other hand, a cash injection could free up your business to do any of the following:

- Offer longer credit terms to your customers to attract more business
- Generally chase more business to increase sales
- Pay off or reduce the amount owed to creditors or the bank

It's important for you to understand the impact on working capital of withdrawing cash from your business. Many small business owners treat the business as their own private bank account and withdraw large amounts of cash on a whim, or buy large capital items without thinking that they are starving the business of working capital. Next time, think before you write that cheque!

"Without doubt 'Cash is King' is the most fundamental phrase for a small business. Keeping a running record of its expenses as well as income is the only way to effectively run the business. It's no fun finding out 6 months after your year-end that the company has huge liabilities and is at risk of going down the pan. Tax liabilities are often not considered. Rather than give your accountant a bag of receipts at the end of the year, hire a bookkeeper and get at least quarterly management accounts."

Phil Hendy ACCA, PHB Accounting, www.wiltshireaccountants.co.uk

You can now see why having a sufficient supply of cash, creditors granting good terms or an overdraft limit, is important. Without the ability to turn debtors or stock into cash quickly enough, the business could starve of cash and die. Unless there is a lot of cash in the system it's vital for a business forced to grant long credit terms and holding slow moving stock to have the back up of an overdraft or creditors.

A business can be profitable on paper in that it has debtors waiting to pay up but the problem is that your true profit (hard, solid cash) is tied up in your debtor book ... you cannot unlock your profit until your debtors pay up. Until then, it's all on paper - the "profit" is useless, it doesn't exist. Without cash, a business can't work. So you can see that even if a business is profitable, it can still fail if its cash isn't flowing properly.

Many profitable businesses have collapsed simply because they ran out of cash.

If you take only two learning points from this book it should be these:

- 'Cash is king'
- 'Turnover is vanity, cash flow is sanity'

For XYZ Ltd, their liquidity position is a strength. There are many companies which run with a net current asset deficit. On a day-to-day basis this doesn't necessarily cause problems as long as creditors and the bank are happy to continue their support. The problems happen when creditors for example suddenly shorten the length of credit they are prepared to give; it changes the make-up or balance of the cycle.

In assessing a set of Financial Statements, the bank will see a lack of liquidity as a weakness, so it is not an issue you can ignore.

Working Capital Ratios

In order to help the Manager assess your liquidity or working capital position, there are a number of ratios he can use which give useful pointers as to the strength or weakness of your liquidity position. As with all such ratios, on their own they don't mean much but when taken as a trend, year-on-year, they can indicate whether a business is moving in the right direction. More importantly, they can prompt questions, enabling the Manager to find out more about how your business works, how actively it's managed and how much you know about your business.

The ratios we will look at are useful for the bank to compare your performance against businesses in a similar industry. If, when compared to every other business in that industry, you are out of line the bank will want to know why. What are you doing differently? Is this having a positive or negative impact on your performance?

Let's look at some of the more commonly used ratios in assessing a business.

Liquidity Ratio

One way to look at liquidity is to compare the trend between the years to see in which direction it's moving i.e. is the business becoming more or less liquid? The Liquidity Ratio calculates the proportion of current assets to current liabilities. It's worked out as follows:

Current Assets / Current Liabilities

Let's look at XYZ's liquid ratio:

20X1:   73,600 / 41,300   =   1.78

20X2:   75,750 / 36,900   =   2.05

Between the two years, XYZ's liquid ratio has improved, so on the face of it their ability to meet day-to-day demands has strengthened to two times cover. This movement has happened because between the two years, current assets have increased and current liabilities have reduced, thereby pushing the ratio in the right direction.

However this doesn't tell you how quickly debtors and stock can be turned into cash. The ratio merely highlights that current assets cover current liabilities by two times. You need to understand the make up of debtors and creditors before you can fully assess your true liquidity position.

The Liquidity Ratio examines liquidity on a high level but there are ratios which break down performance into even greater detail by assessing the individual components of current assets and current liabilities.

Debtor Collection Ratio

This ratio assesses how efficiently debtors are collected and is based on how many days on average it takes the business to collect its debts. The ratio is worked out as follows:

Debtors / Sales x 365 days

XYZ's ratios would be:

20X1:   15,600 / 425,000 x 365   =   13 days

20X2:   21,300 / 450,000 x 365   =   17 days

In the first year, on average it took XYZ 13 days to collect its debtors. However, by the second year, this had worsened to 17 days. Why? The bank will want to find out what has happened because such fall can have an impact on XYZ's cash flow - the fall in collection days means cash is not being generated as quickly as before.

There could be a number of reasons for the change:

- Business increased so much that the owner of XYZ has become lax in debtor collection.

- The accounts department may have lost an important person and efficiency has suffered.

- It may be a specific change of policy i.e. in order to attract more business, longer credit terms were offered in year two. In this case the slippage can be seen in a positive light as long as the effect on cash flow and the working capital cycle has been understood and planned for.

- There could be long outstanding debtors which are distorting the ratio. For example a debtor may be suffering from financial problems and not paid up. This can increase the average number of days. To better understand if this is the case, the Manager could ask to see an aged analysis of XYZ's debtor book. An analysis categorises the money owed into time buckets of invoices outstanding for less than 30 days, 60 days and over 90 days. Analysing your debtor portfolio in this way is a good test of the efficiency of your collection process.

Problems with an inefficient debt collection process can lead to severe cash flow difficulties. A slippage in debtor collection days should be a prompt to look at your systems to see if it can be improved and this may include looking at outsourcing your collection process.

"People set up a new business venture for a number of reasons but few realise how difficult and time-consuming it can be to chase for payment of invoices. Cash needs to be released from your debtor portfolio on a consistent basis to keep your business moving and an outsourced invoicing service can help you achieve this efficiently and cost-effectively.

Many of your clients will no doubt be experiencing financial hardship and it is often a case that they avoid making payments unless they are chased. An outsourced invoicing service will do this in a friendly but efficient manner to ensure that your hard earned relationship is not compromised. You will have all the benefits of a finance department, but without the cost, ensuring that your invoices are paid promptly and minimising the risk of bad debts.

An outsourced invoicing service can help you free up your time, improve your cash flow, keep your Bank Manager happy and let you concentrate on growing your business."

Andrew Witts, Hate Invoicing, www.hateinvoicing.com

Obviously by looking at the overall debtor total we don't know how well spread the number of debtors are. By 'spread' I'm referring to how many individual debtors there are in total; the higher the number of individual debtors, then the less likely the business is to be affected if one debtor fails to pay up. So, assuming payments due are of similar amounts, a debtor book of 100 names is well spread. A debtor book spread over only 3 names could make the business vulnerable.

The wider the spread of names, the better protected your business is.

It isn't necessarily a bad sign if the ratio does change, either up or down; it may be a planned strategy and that is why any change in trend has to be examined and questions asked to get to the root cause of the shift.

Creditor Payment Ratio

This ratio assesses how many days on average it takes the business to pay its creditors. It's worked out as follows:

Creditors / Purchases x   365 days

XYZ's ratios would be:

20X1:	30,900 / 210,450 x 365	=	54 days
20X2:	22,400 / 229,580 x 365	=	36 days

During the first year on average XYZ paid their creditors within 54 days. By year 2, this has changed to 36 days. Again, as with the debtor collection period, the question is, why the change?

In year 1 XYZ paid suppliers within 54 days and so the business could make use of the cash preserved by the long credit terms to fund stock purchases or balance out longer credit terms given to their customers. In year 2, the company paid off creditors much quicker, which meant that cash within the business was being used up faster than before. Why did they do this?

The change in policy to speed up payments could be due to a number of reasons:

- Suppliers could have revised their terms of credit downwards thereby forcing XYZ to pay up quicker.

- XYZ may have found themselves in a better cash position than in the previous year and decided to pay off creditors quicker than the previous year to perhaps enhance their reputation with suppliers or to access higher credit limits.

- XYZ may be doing business with a new supplier whose terms are significantly lower than other suppliers so bringing down the average number of days taken to pay.
- The 20X1 ratio of 54 days may have been artificially inflated due to a distortion caused by one large bill. The bill could have been under dispute and so remained unpaid. By 20X2, this may have been paid so returning the ratio to a more normal figure.

If the ratio had worsened, with the number of days taken to settle creditors having increased, this could be attributed to:

- Suppliers voluntarily revising their terms of credit upwards thereby giving XYZ more time to pay at no extra cost.
- XYZ may have found themselves in a tighter cash position than in the previous year and decided to take full advantage of credit terms on offer, whereas in previous years they paid off quicker than was required.
- XYZ may be doing business with a new supplier whose terms are significantly different from other suppliers so increasing the average number of days taken to pay.
- A long outstanding creditor may be distorting the figure. The underlying contract could be in dispute and so is not being settled.

If the number of days taken to pay is reducing then the bank won't be too concerned as long as the quicker use of cash is not straining cash flow. If it is moving in the opposite direction then the bank is likely to ask questions in case this is an early sign of a cash crisis i.e. the business is delaying settling its creditors because of lack of cash.

To reassure himself, your Manager could ask you to provide an aged analysis of your creditors, along the same lines as the debtor book analysis. Outstanding creditors for over, say, 3 months will be looked at and questioned as to why they have not been paid. It could be as simple as one purchase was negotiated with a longer credit period than usual or the purchase could be under dispute.

Analysis of the creditor book will also give the Manager a feel for how well spread your creditors are. As with debtors, having just 3 creditors can put the business in a vulnerable position; if one creditor demands immediate repayment would you be able to pay? However, if creditors are well spread the chances of one bringing the business down is unlikely (unless in amount terms that particular payment is significant.)

As ever, the reason can only be found out if questions are asked to clarify apparent trends.

Stock Turnover Ratio

This ratio shows how quickly stock in the business turns over, i.e. how many days it takes to move stock out of the business. It's worked out as follows:

Closing Stock / Sales x 365

XYZ's ratio would be:

20X1:	56,700 / 425,000 x 365	=	49 days
20X2:	53,400 / 450,000 x 365	=	43 days

This indicates that in year 1, XYZ sold its stock on average every 49 days. In year 2 the ratio had improved in that stock was selling every 43 days. Cash has been released quicker into the business than in the previous year. This improvement could be down to a number of reasons:

- Despite sales increasing, the amount of stock held in order to meet those sales was not increased in proportion. This may have been a deliberate policy to reduce the amount of cash tied up in stock.
- There may have been a stock clear out which removed previously slow moving stock thereby improving the ratio.

- A new, faster moving range of stock may have been introduced, thereby bringing the ratio down.

Either way, for XYZ their cash position will have improved because they are turning stock into cash much faster than before and keeping a tighter control on stock. However, a possible effect on customer service has to be taken into consideration. Have reduced stock levels impacted on delivery times? Have stock levels fallen so far that the business is failing to deliver on customer expectations? How many times have you been frustrated when told by a furniture shop that your new sofa will take six weeks before delivery? The furniture industry has understood the impact on cash flow of holding relatively high ticket items readily available in the stockroom.

The ratio moving in the opposite direction, with more stock being held in relation to sales, naturally has a negative impact on cash flow. As with debtors and creditors, this ratio can be distorted by long unsold stock or a shift in stock holding policy, so the bank may ask for more details on stock holding to see if there is stock which is effectively unsaleable. If there is, the bank may reduce the total stock valuation figure by the unsaleable stock value to come up with a more reliable figure.

Working Capital Ratio

This useful ratio can assess how much additional working capital is needed per £000 increase in sales. It's only a rough guide based on the performance of the year in question but it is a useful quick assessment guide and will give you an indication as to how much cash you would need to fund any expected increase in sales. It's worked out as follows:

Working Capital* / Sales

*working capital = current assets less current liabilities

Let's have a look at XYZ's working capital ratio in 20X2:

working capital = £75,750 - £36,900 =   £38,850

£38,850 / £450,000 x 1000 = £86

This ratio tells us that XYZ would need an additional £86 of working capital for each £1000 of additional sales. So, if they were looking to increase sales by £150,000 they would need extra working capital of £12,900. This could be financed by:

- A cash injection from the Directors
- An increase in its overdraft facility
- An increase in credit terms from suppliers
- Reducing credit terms given to customers
- Selling stock quicker

This is a very helpful ratio and will give you a quick indication as to whether you need additional support from your bank or a cash injection into the business.

Trends and Questions

As with all of the ratios we have looked at, one year's figures do not mean much; it's the trend between years which tell the story and prompt questions. These ratios can give further indications as to whether the business is well managed or if there is room for improvement. The ratios help add to the overall picture the bank is building up about your business. In isolation the ratios can only tell you so much, but backed with explanations they can be very powerful.

If you can present explanations as to why certain ratios have moved then this can only impress the Manager; it shows you are in control and that you know what's going on within your business.

So dig out your Financial Statements, take some time and calculate your working capital ratios; it will give you a better understanding of how your business works.

Remember that in each case the bank will be rating your ratio performance and trends as either a strength or weakness. Each of the ratio assessments will go towards the overall assessment of your performance and financial strength.

PROFIT AND LOSS ASSESSMENT – ARE YOU MAKING ANY MONEY?

The aim of every business owner should naturally be to make money. If you are driven by this philosophy (and I hope you are) it's important that you continually assess how profitable your business is and to track trends from year to year.

As with a Balance Sheet there are a number of useful measures and ratios which can be used to assess where a business stands.

Sales Growth

Ideally every business needs to see its sales increase year on year. For top class performance this growth has to be an increase in "real" terms, i.e. growth after inflation has been taken into account. For example, a 2% increase in sales when inflation is running at 3% means that in real terms, growth has been negative. Growth in excess of inflation should be the target.

If this has not been achieved, then the business has either stood still or, even worse, gone into reverse. If there has been flat growth the bank is going to want to know what you are doing to change that trend. All of this must be covered in your Business Plan.

Looking at XYZ's accounts you will see that sales increase was 5% in 20X2. Until we know what the inflation rate was during that year

PROFIT AND LOSS FOR XYZ LTD
31ST DECEMBER 200X1 AND 20X2

	20X1			20X2	
Sales		425,000		450,000	
Opening Stock	-54,300		-56,700		
Purchases	-210,450		-229,580		
Closing Stock	56,700		53,400		
Cost of Sales	-208,050		-232,880		
Gross Profit		216,950		217,120	
Overheads					
Salaries	76,500		80,450		
Directors' Salaries	59,950		66,700		
Electricity	2,300		2,100		
Rent, Rates, Water	3,300		3,550		
Stationery, Printing	2,450		2,600		
Insurance	4,400		4,600		
Repairs, Renewals	2,700		5,100		
Telephone	950		970		
Travel	1,950		1,700		
Postage	750		850		
Bank Charges	1,200		1,450		
Bank Interest	7,400		6,650		
Depreciation	22,000	185,850	20,000	196,720	
Net Profit		31,100		20,400	

we are unable to say whether the business is an eagle or a turkey. Progress certainly, but either way, not that staggering.

In assessing an increase in sales you must take into consideration whether it has been achieved by merely hiking up the unit price. This will have the effect of increasing headline income but leaving the number of units sold exactly the same; good for a short term gain but not necessarily good for the long term - there will be a time when this strategy won't work any more.

The bank will be looking to see that sales growth is being actively managed and that positive, proactive headway is being made.

Gross Profit Percentage

This ratio calculates the profit in percentage terms that the business is making on sales, after the cost of the raw materials or stock is deducted. It demonstrates how efficiently the business has been producing its goods year by year. The ideal position is that the gross profit margin increases each year. The figure is calculated as follows:

Gross Profit / Sales x 100

XYZ's gross profit percentage is:

20X1:   216,950 / 425,000 x 100   =   51%

20X2:   217,120 / 450,000 x 100   =   48%

XYZ's gross profit percentage dropped from 51% to 48%. As with all the other ratios, the bank will need to understand the reason behind the fall. There could be a number of reasons for this drop:

- In order to stimulate sales, the company may have reduced prices either permanently or as part of a specific marketing campaign. This would have had a negative impact on gross profit percentage, although in monetary terms it will have led to an increase in gross profit because of the increase in sales. This strategy can backfire in that sales may not respond to the downward revision in prices, so if you are going down this route you have to be sure of your market and how it will react.

- XYZ may have paid more for their raw materials or stock during 20X2 perhaps to secure better quality or just because of a general price increase. If they could not pass this price increase onto their customers then margins would have suffered. Ideally XYZ has to demonstrate that a specific policy decision was taken not to pass on the price increase. It shows that the business is being actively managed with policy not being dictated by outside influences.

Asking a business owner what he did during the year to influence his gross profit percentage, or what happened which was outside of his control, is a good way for the bank to assess the owner's grip on the business. What would your answer be?

Overheads as a Percentage of Sales

This ratio looks at the relationship between overheads and sales. The ideal position is that as sales increase, overheads as a percentage of sales either remain static or reduce. This demonstrates the control the business has on overheads and is an indication of the business' ongoing efficiency. If overheads as a percentage of sales keep going up year by year, it suggests that cost controls have slipped and that the business is not being run as efficiently as before.

The ratio is worked out as follows:

Overheads / Sales x 100

XYZ's figures look like this:

20X1:   185,850 / 425,000 x 100   =   43.7%

20X2:   196,720 / 450,000 x 100   =   43.7%

XYZ has done well; sales increased by nearly 6% yet overheads have remained at a constant level. This means that the business has coped with an increase in sales without having to increase overheads as a proportion of that increase. It demonstrates that in year 2 they have been relatively efficient. But notice that there was an increase in Directors' Salaries – always a good one for a banker to look at and question.

Net Profit Percentage

This calculation indicates the overall profitability of the business after taking into account sales, gross profit and overheads. It's calculated as follows:

Net Profit / Sales x 100

XYZ's performance is:

20X1:	31,100 / 425,000 x 100	=	7.3%
20X2:	20,400 / 450,000 x 100	=	4.5%

Not a good performance by XYZ. Despite sales increasing net profit was down. This was due to two factors:

- The contribution towards overheads in the form of gross profit was not enough. Despite the sales increase of £25,000, gross profit only increased by £170.

- Although overheads as a percentage of sales remained static, there was still a cash increase in overheads of £10,870 (if you include depreciation which is not strictly a cash deduction – a point we will look at later). With the low increase in gross profit this resulted in a lower profit than the previous year.

You can see from this figure that going for growth in sales doesn't necessarily translate into an increase in profits. In XYZ's case, the problem appears to be at the cost of goods/raw materials level.

What can they do to get back on track?

Interest Cover

This ratio shows how much profit the business has generated in order to meet interest costs. It's worked out based on the number of times Profit Before Interest covers the interest being charged. It's calculated as follows:

Profit Before Interest* / Interest

* net profit plus interest

XYZ's interest cover would be:

20X1:	38,500 / 7,400	=	5.2
20X2:	27,050 / 6,650	=	4.0

XYZ has a healthy 5.2 times interest cover in 20X1 and 4 times in 20X2. The fall in cover in the second year is of concern but with this much interest cover there shouldn't be a problem. Having high interest cover provides comfort and makes the business less vulnerable to any sudden upward movements in interest rates.

These profit-related ratios are useful to assess a business' efficiency, especially when the year-on-year trends are reviewed. From the bank's perspective the key is asking questions about the trends to gain a better understanding of the business.

Work out your ratios and see what conclusions you can draw from them.

SERVICEABILITY ASSESSMENT – CAN YOU PAY THE BANK BACK?

In agreeing to lend to you the bank has to be comfortable that you are able to pay back your loan or cover the interest on your overdraft. This is referred to as serviceability – can your business service its debts? In the current climate, and going forward, banks are now going back to basics and strongly testing a business' ability to service its debts.

In this, the final of the four assessment areas, there are a number of tools available to help your Manager satisfy himself that your facility is serviceable.

Break-even Analysis

In any business there is a point at which neither a profit or a loss is made. This is called the break-even point, i.e. the point to which sales can fall before a loss is made or the point to where sales have to rise before a profit is made. Once the break-even point is reached, each unit sold thereafter makes a profit contribution. It's important for any business to know its break-even point.

However, before being able to work out the break-even point, you have to understand the concept of fixed and variable costs.

Fixed Costs

Fixed costs are overheads that have to be met regardless of whether sales are made or not. Fixed costs are expenses which do not vary when sales go up or down; you will have to pay them regardless of what level your sales are at.

If you are running a shop, for example, your fixed costs would include:

- Rent and rates
- Electricity - you have to keep the lights on to attract customers into the shop
- Wages for one member of staff, or even for yourself
- Insurance
- Depreciation (although this is a non-cash item, it is regarded as a fixed cost)

Variable Costs

Variable costs are expenses that fluctuate according to the level of trading. As sales increase so will your variable costs. Conversely, when sales fall these expenses will also fall.

Examples of variable costs would be:

- Raw materials and stock - as sales increase you have to buy in more materials or stock in order to meet the increased demand. This is the most common variable cost.
- Casual labour - most salaries are considered as fixed costs but if you employ casual labour to meet rush orders then this is a variable cost.
- Stationery, telephone etc. As we will see later, some of these are semi-fixed but taken as variable costs.

Break-even is achieved when a business has generated enough gross profit to meet its fixed costs and variable costs. Unless they generate sufficient sales or curb costs then the business will be loss-making.

Break-even is worked out as follows:

Fixed Costs / Contribution* x Sales

*Contribution = Sales less Variable Costs (contribution is effectively what is left over, after variable costs have been met, to meet fixed costs)

To calculate your break-even point first go through your Financial Statements or projections and categorise your costs into fixed and variable costs. Consider each cost and ask yourself these two questions:

Question 1:

"Even if I only had one customer, would I still have to pay this cost?"

If yes, then it is a fixed cost

Question 2:

"Will this cost increase if my sales increase?"

If yes, then it is a variable cost.

There are some costs which can have an element of being both fixed and variable, for example, electricity; an element of the bill is fixed but at the same time usage may go up as sales increase - this depends on your line of business. It's just a case of taking a view when you're splitting everything out.

However, if you are comparing your break-even year-by-year on a basis of trends the trick is to be consistent in your definition of fixed and variable otherwise you won't be comparing like-with-like. So if you decide that because you are a manufacturer your electricity costs will be variable, then in future years' calculations keep it this way.

Having done this exercise you can then work out your break-even sales figure and identify what your margin of error is in terms of sales before you start making losses i.e. how far your sales can drop before you're into loss-making territory, or if you want to think positively, at what level of sales do you start making a profit!

XYZ's Break-Even

Let's have a look at XYZ's break-even for 20X1. Having gone through the figures I reckon its fixed costs would be made up of:

- Salaries
- Directors' salaries
- Electricity
- Rent, rates and water
- Insurance
- Depreciation.

All of this comes to £168,450. The variable costs are the remainder and these total £225,450. Its break-even would therefore be:

Contribution: £425,000 - £225,450 = £199,550

168,450 / 199,550 x 425,000 = £358,763

For XYZ, their break-even in 20X1 was £358,763. In other words they have to achieve this level of sales if they are to neither make a profit or a loss.

XYZ could see its sales drop from its 20X1 level by 16% before a loss is incurred. For many businesses this margin of safety may be too thin and they could set themselves a target to widen the margin.

Break-even is a relatively easy calculation to work out and so is worthwhile doing. There can be a number of grey areas where allocation of fixed and variable costs are concerned but it's a case of looking at each individual business and deciding from there.

For the bank, this is a useful calculation because it shows how close a business is to loss-making and how much leeway a business has before it starts incurring losses. A consistent run of losses will put the serviceability of any borrowing in doubt.

Profit Surplus

In assessing a request for finance the bank needs to work out whether the business can afford the loan repayments or to cover the interest charges on the overdraft. As well as looking at the financial projections or forecasts, which are the main source of confirmation that banks look to for comfort, the bank can also look at past performance.

By looking at the previous year's profit figure and adding back depreciation, which is not a cash item (at the end of the financial year you don't write out a cheque made payable to "depreciation"), you arrive at the true cash profit the business made during the year.

In XYZ's case the surplus in 20X2 was £40,400, which is the net profit of £20,400 and depreciation of £20,000 added back. If XYZ has requested a loan which involves monthly repayments of £1,000 or £12,000 per annum, then they appear to have the cash profit available to service the loan, assuming there are no major changes in the company's finances going forward.

Remember though that profit does not equal cash. On paper you can be profitable but cash flow is what it's all about. So, although on the face of it the business may have the profit to meet any repayments, it may not have the physical cash, which is where the cash flow projection comes in. The projections, which will be included in the Business Plan, are important because they forecast ahead and so are more representative than past performance.

XZY'S Overall Financial Position

What about XYZ's position? Overall, there are some good points and some bad points, or perhaps better said as "areas of concern"!

There is nothing fundamentally wrong but the business has to look at maximising the potential of its sales growth by aiming for a much higher growth in real terms; they have to concentrate on increasing their margins and review overheads. At the end of the day the business is strong with a good track record of retained profits and a growing Net Worth.

In assessing any request for finance, the bank would consider XYZ's financial position as a strength.

What About Your Business?

I have given you all the key information on how to read a Profit and Loss statement and Balance Sheet, so set aside some time to review the various ratios we have looked at in respect of your business. Examine your overall financial performance to identify your areas of strengths and weaknesses. It will be time well spent. As well as getting to know your business it will give you the edge during the assessment process because at least you'll know what the Manager is talking about!

We have now finished our look at the areas which the bank would consider when examining a Balance Sheet and Profit and Loss account, and you can see that there's a lot to review.

Whilst the Accounts are historic and so won't reflect any future changes planned within the business, it will give a good indication of the likelihood of future success, so it's worthwhile examining them in addition to the projections.

We have seen that taken in isolation, the figures mean little; the power is when you compare year-to-year and examine the movements or trends. These movements prompt questions which, when answered, provide the bank with more insight into the business. Armed with the knowledge on how to read Accounts you will now be better prepared for the questions the bank is likely to ask.

Analysis of the Accounts is only one part of the process of reviewing a request for finance. Next we will look at other factors which are taken into consideration.

Phew – that's the numbers bit finished … you can now breathe easy!!

THE CREDIT ASSESSMENT FRAMEWORK

Having looked at how the bank reviews your Financial Statements we will now consider the many other factors which the bank will consider when assessing your request for a loan or overdraft.

Each bank will have its own method or style of reviewing a request for finance but the basics are the same and essentially revolve around two questions:

"Is our money safe? Will it be repaid on time based on the information we have on this client?"

The use of computer models to analyse past behaviour and so predict future behaviour has modernised the assessment process. Your request is very likely to pass through a computer first for an initial review as to whether it fits the bank's credit policy. However, the basics remain sound and form the fundamental building blocks of an automated review process.

Before we start it's worth reiterating some points I covered in the Introduction to this book. Over the past few years the whole assessment process has been thrown out of the window. Common sense did not, in many cases, prevail. This will change and we will start to see a return to normality, but not the normality you may think of. What we saw during the boom years was not normal and what we are going to see is a 'back to basics' approach of banks getting to know your business better with a keen focus on demonstrating serviceability.

What we will go through now is the simplest and best way to understand the Bank Manager's thought process.

A Structured Approach

Your Business Plan is a very structured document; there are clear sections, each dealing with separate issues and giving the reader an understanding of your business.

Your Business Plan, the review of your Financial Statements and what he has gleaned from his interview with you will have provided your Manager with a wealth of material about you and your business. All of this will be used in the evaluation process.

Just as your Plan is structured, so is the process of assessing your request. The Plan and the interview will have contained so much information that it can be difficult to put it into a sensible order. A structured approach allows a more formal assessment of the viability of the proposal and helps guide the Manager in making the right decision.

Assessment Frameworks

The frameworks used (each bank tends to use a different version but essentially looking at the same issues) are based around a similar set of questions or issues which need to be considered when a request for finance is being reviewed.

In giving you an insight into the Manager's thought processes we are going to look in depth at the more commonly used frameworks which work well together and are put into useful mnemonics:

1. CAMPARI

2. SWOT

3. LEPEST

These three frameworks fit the small business sector perfectly. They consider the request for support from the angle of both the individual behind the business, the business itself and the market it operates in. Banks won't be using these frameworks directly but they neatly sum up the key considerations when making a lending assessment.

Let's have a brief overview of each before we go into them in more depth.

CAMPARI

Developed in the 1970s, each of these letters stands for a part of the assessment process:

CHARACTER

ABILITY

MARGIN

PURPOSE

AMOUNT

REPAYMENT

INSURANCE

Each aspect of the mnemonic covers a different part of the business and it helps guide the assessor down a particular route and ensures that every facet of the request is reviewed. By using this framework, nothing is missed and it is an ideal way for you to grasp the areas of your business bankers will be focusing on.

SWOT Analysis

To back up CAMPARI there is another mnemonic which adds an additional perspective to the analysis process. This is the better known mnemonic, SWOT, the darling of all business courses and seminars. The reason it's so popular is that it works!

SWOT stands for:

STRENGTHS

WEAKNESSES

OPPORTUNITIES

THREATS

Strengths and weaknesses are internal factors affecting the business, which can be controlled or influenced by the management of the company. For example, a well-trained workforce would be assessed as a strength, as would a good financial controls policy. On the flip side a non-existent marketing strategy or poor staff relations experience would be seen as a weakness.

However, it is not only internal policies that can affect the business; external factors which are out of the company's sphere of influence or control can also impact on business performance. These factors and their impact are assessed as either an opportunity or a threat. For example, a previously strong competitor is closing down - this would be seen as an opportunity for you because their customers will now be looking for a new 'home'. Other opportunities may lie in the introduction of a new product in response to changing market needs or demands. A threat may be that new legislation is being introduced which may damage the business, or your industry is being targeted as a contributor to global warming.

As we saw when analysing Financial Statements, each aspect of a business can be assessed as a strength or weakness and so it is with CAMPARI; each key area forming the CAMPARI mnemonic can be assessed as a strength or weakness. This helps build up a picture of the business - whether it's strong or weak.

The opportunities and threats part of the SWOT completes the picture by looking at the external influences affecting the business. To provide a guideline as to what are the external opportunities and threats the LEPEST framework can be used.

LEPEST Analysis

The LEPEST framework considers the various issues which can affect the business and yet are outside its sphere of influence – the event will happen come what may and you can do nothing to change it. But what could those events be?

LEPEST stands for:

LEGAL

ENVIRONMENTAL

POLITICAL

ECONOMIC

SOCIOLOGICAL

TECHNOLOGICAL

Each of these issues can negatively or positively impact your business. To make a complete assessment of your business the bank needs to consider how each of these issues could affect the safety of its lending.

We will look at SWOT and LEPEST in more depth later but for now we will move on to look at each element of CAMPARI and see how it is a useful summary of the factors making up the assessment process.

CAMPARI – CHARACTER

It's important for any small business entrepreneur to understand that the bank is not lending to your business but to you. This is not the case where large companies are concerned but it certainly rings true with small and medium sized enterprises:

- *You* are the business
- *You* make the decisions
- *You* choose the direction
- *You* make the money

Too many small business owners think there is a clear dividing line between them and their business but in reality you are inextricably linked. It's fitting therefore that CAMPARI starts with character, or the person behind the business, the one who could lead the business down the road of success or failure!

"Banks lend to people not plans. Once, visiting a bank with a client and the plan we had done together, the bank manager said, "Mr Wright, we are not lending to you, we are lending to Mr X your client. Let him answer the questions unless you are planning to be his business partner."

A business plan needs to be good enough to be considered but thereafter it is up to the business owner to convince the bank manager they can deliver the plan and have the personal qualities and financial record to be trusted with a loan.

It pays to be upfront and honest about a "damaged" credit history.

In my experience banks prefer to lend to a team, if only of two, than a single business owner. Statistics indicate that businesses with 2 or more partners / owners are more likely to succeed than a one man band.

In one case we dropped one of the three business promoters from being a director because his damaged credit history resulted in low points with a bank's credit scoring."

Albert Wright, Small Business Solutions Ltd, www.sbsltd.net

The bank has to be happy that the owner has the right background and commitment to make a success of the business. Ultimately, even if you have the best product on the market, this is of no significance if you are deemed to be a poor risk and can't be trusted with the bank's money.

So, what aspects of a person's character are considered?

What Is Your Age and Health?

Like it or not, age has to be a factor in the credit assessment. If a businessman, particularly a one man band operation, asks for a loan repayable over 25 years and he's already 70, the chances of him being around to see full repayment are pretty slim!

You may be the key person within the business who makes it all tick. Yes, you may be fighting fit for your age but your loss, either through long-term sickness or death, may have a negative impact on business performance and hence the safety of the bank's money.

On the other hand, a spotty-faced 18 year old just out of school asking for £100,000 may not be considered a strength either! Age is not a major problem but if you are at either end of the age scale then it is an issue to be taken into consideration.

Equally, your health also has a bearing on how the potential success of your venture is assessed. Someone who is clearly on his last legs may not be considered a good risk!

You won't find the Manager asking for your doctor's report or delving into your past illnesses though; his thoughts and findings will be based on what he can see and already knows.

What Was The Source of Introduction?

In preparing your Business Plan you may decide you don't want to present it to your current bank. This may be for a number of reasons:

- You don't like the level of service you're currently experiencing
- You may have had a chequered past with them and you want a fresh start
- Your bank may not be conveniently located near your business and now is the time to look for a new banking partner

If you don't hold an account with the bank you're approaching, and this is your first contact, the Manager will want to know why you aren't approaching your own bank. Have they already turned you down? If so, why? What do they know that he doesn't? All these questions will be going through his mind.

If your own bank has turned you down be up front and tell them. In some circumstances personality clashes between the business owner and the Manager can happen and unfortunately cloud the decision-making process when a new request is presented. So be up front about the reasons as to why you are casting your net wider.

Having made the decision to refer your Plan elsewhere, you have two options: you can either turn up cold at the bank of your choice, or you could ask a business colleague to introduce you to their bank (assuming they are happy with the service they are getting). If he knows you and the skills you possess, he may be prepared to do more than point you in the right direction; he may be happy to "vouch" for you. By doing this, he's telling his Manager that, in his opinion, you have a good chance of success and are worthy of support.

If your colleague is a respected businessman, has a good reputation and operates a well conducted account, then this type of introduction could be considered a strength.

An alternative source of introduction could be your accountant or solicitor. They usually have good contacts within the banking industry and an introduction from them can go a long way. However, they have professional reputations to protect, so they will only assist you if they have reviewed your Plan and are convinced you have a good chance of success.

If you can't find anyone to introduce you and you have to go in cold then don't worry, it's not a problem. Conversely, an introduction from someone else doesn't guarantee you success either!

What Are The Business and Personal Assets?

During the interview the Manager is likely to ask for details of the assets you own and what your liabilities are, so you may as well prepare a personal statement of your assets and liabilities. The reason for wanting to know your worth as an individual goes back to the point that the smaller the business is, the more the bank is lending to you as an individual, and so your personal financial background is relevant and important.

This sort of information can give a useful insight into someone's character. If you own your own home, are married and have 2.4 children then you are seen as a stable, someone-you-can-rely-on type of person. (I am sure there are many of you who would disagree with that, but it's the way of the world!)

Having a mortgage and a car loan are all strengths, assuming that the monthly repayments are not out of line when compared to your income. Why does having a mortgage or other loans help your case? A mortgage is a sign of stability; people with mortgages don't ordinarily walk away from things. Also, another financial institution has deemed you fit enough to lend to, so that's a stamp of approval. However, if you had a mortgage but it has been paid off, leaving your house debt free, then that's even better; it's an asset, which is available to raise cash against in the future, if necessary.

Savings, in the form of cash or shares, shows you have the discipline to put money aside and plan your finances accordingly. Even if you're not putting all your savings into the business as your stake, it's wise to reveal these in the interview because savings are considered to be a strength. However, if you have built up a good asset base purely on the back of a rise in house prices, and nothing through regular savings, then this can be a downside - you've increased your personal wealth by doing nothing.

Age comes into it as well. Someone with a reasonable income and no savings by the time they reach their 30s can seem a bit questionable. Alternatively, this would not be expected for someone in their earlier 20s. If there are legitimate reasons for not having savings behind you, make sure you explain why.

As I mentioned previously, if you are a one man band or a small operation, then the bank is lending to you, not the business, and so share the details of your personal worth. All of these financial issues help draw up a picture of who you are.

Naturally, if you are already in business then the business itself will have accumulated assets. This can be in the form of buildings, stock and debtors. A business which has been in existence for 10 years and has built up next to nothing in the form of assets will not score well. On the other hand, a business which has been around for only 3 years and yet has built up an impressive asset base will score positively.

What Does The Credit Search or Business Credit Report Reveal?

As we saw in the section on what you need to do to open a bank account, the bank will do a credit search to see what is listed against you such as CCJs (County Court Judgements), searches undertaken by other financial institutions or bankruptcy notices. Whilst they will have done this when you opened your account, new entries are added all the time so an up to date search will be undertaken when you apply for a facility.

If you have ever defaulted on a loan, catalogue payment or any other financial contract, the company involved will probably have lodged a default against your name and address (if they have entered into an agreement with credit reference agencies to supply such information), so don't think that such a thing is forgotten - it's not. This acts as a warning to other lenders that you have not honoured previous obligations and this won't go in your favour.

If you trade via a Limited Company the bank can order a Business Credit Report which provides similar details to a search against an individual. One of the differences though is that participating companies can log data with the credit reference agency as to how promptly you settle their invoices – a good source of information for the bank if they are looking to advance you money!

"If your business is already established and you are trading as a Limited Company then the bank may request a Business Credit Report from one of the credit bureaux.

As with the consumer credit report which provides information on you as an individual, the business report will provide details on your Limited Company's background which includes:

- *Financial performance for the last 5 years;*
- *An adverse check for all CCJs registered against the business, the value, which court, and whether settled or not;*
- *Some of the bureaux also provide a payment profile which is extracted from hundreds of ledgers provided by participating companies, and outlines their trading experiences with you if they supply on credit terms. This element of the report will reveal either a good payment record or a 'bad days beyond terms' payment record, by age, value and number of experiences.*

As with your personal adverse history, you cannot hide from this so be upfront with your lender.

Before approaching a lender ensure all of your company and director details are correct. If incorrect there will be a delay whilst these details are checked and corrected.

By combining historical financial data and the live information that is available, the bureau will then rely on their scoring model to provide an accurate assessment of your business' general creditworthiness."

Kevin Duggan, Check2Cheque Ltd
www.check2cheque.co.uk

If there is anything registered against you, be up front about it; admitting it early on in the process will do you more favours than trying to conveniently forget about it. The bank *will* search and it *will* be brought up in discussions. A poor credit search or report will be classed as a weakness but the impact may not be so bad if you are up front and explain the background. Mention it before the bank does.

Something to bear in mind is that each time a financial institution does a credit search their enquiry is registered, so when another company does a search, all the previous searches come up. If, in the last month, there are five banks or leasing companies who have carried out searches against you, the Manager will want to know about the sudden flurry of activity. It could mean you are merely touting your request around to see who will give you the best deal. On the other hand, it could mean that you have been unsuccessful in getting help and this bank is the next one on the list.

Unfortunately there are very few things you can hide in this age of "Big Brother"! Anything registered against you will be regarded as a weakness unless there is a very good explanation for the entry. I have seen a number of people who have defaults or judgements registered due to non-payment of debts because the quality of the goods supplied was poor and payment was withheld. This is perfectly acceptable but make sure you explain the background, preferably backed up with documentary evidence.

There are many cases, though, where people don't realise they have a default registered against them. The financial help pages in the newspapers are littered with people who have discovered an entry relating to a dispute over a poorly fitted carpet! Companies are quick to file these entries so before approaching your bank for finance, it may be worth your while doing a search yourself.

What Is Your Previous Banking History?

How you operate your bank account is a good indicator of how you manage your finances and so is a useful source of information. Your Manager has two options: if you already bank with her she can review your account performance from the bank's records. If you bank elsewhere then she will want to review your account by asking for copies of 6 months' bank statements.

What to Look For

There are a number of things the bank looks for which facilitate building a picture as to how you manage your finances:

- Has your account operated in credit or within the agreed overdraft limit?

- If your account has gone overdrawn or breached the overdraft limit, was it with the bank's agreement, or was it done without arrangement? If the latter, then it's not a good sign as to how you control your finances.

- Have cheques been returned unpaid? If you have had cheques unpaid then this could indicate 2 things:

  o you don't monitor your finances very well in that you issue cheques when there is no money on the account;

  o the bank doesn't consider you a good enough risk, in that it doesn't allow your account to go overdrawn at all.

Both of these points are warning signs. A small number of cheques returned unpaid can be put down to one-off factors but a regular occurrence will be a black mark against you.

- Are cheques being issued in round amounts? If so this may indicate that you can't afford to settle the full invoiced amount, so a portion of it is paid with the remainder being paid off over time. This is evidence of financial pressure. There may be a very good reason why you do this. If so, explain your reasons.

- Do the statements show that cheques are regularly being stopped to avoid payment? This may indicate that you issued cheques but realised too late that there was insufficient money available. Instead of suffering the embarrassment of having the cheques returned unpaid, you get there first and instruct the bank to stop payment.

- As with cheques being returned unpaid, the odd occurrence of cheques being stopped is understandable but regular requests are not. I have seen a number of businesses doing this on a frequent basis and eventually they have been warned to stop the practice or have their account closed.

- Has the nature of the way the account has operated changed over the previous twelve months? If twelve months ago the amount paid in each month was £100,000 but it is now £60,000, there are three possibilities:
  - Sales turnover is down;
  - Cash is not being paid in (perhaps paying creditors direct);
  - The business has opened a bank account elsewhere.

Either way, the bank will want an explanation.

- Do the amounts being paid in and out of the account each year correspond with that reported in the Financial Statements? If sales, for example, are shown as £150,000 but only £50,000 finds its way into the bank account then this needs to be explained. If the figures don't tally, is there another bank account, which has not been revealed?

- Have previous loans been paid off satisfactorily? If so, this is an indication that you are a reasonable credit risk.

- If you have an overdraft, is the average overdrawn balance increasing each month? If you operate in credit, is the credit balance slowly reducing? It could be that you are undertaking a capital expenditure programme and so utilising your working capital (not a good idea, as we discussed earlier).

How to Assess Account Behaviour

Having month-by-month statistics on the operation of your account can help the bank in answering some of the questions we have just looked at. If you have an account at the bank you have approached, then they will have immediate access to information on how your account has operated. If you are with another bank the Manager can manually construct the information by extracting it from the bank statements you will have provided.

Reviewing your bank statements could reveal, for example, that your average overdrawn balance is increasing month-by-month. On the face of it, this is not a good trend and could suggest that losses are being made. However, there may be other good reasons for this trend. For example:

- You may have been building an extension to your factory, or undertaking other capital expenditure and using the overdraft to finance it.

- You could be building up stock in anticipation of a large order.

- Your business may be seasonal and so an increase in your overdraft balance may be expected during that time of year.

As we saw when reviewing Financial Statements it's all about asking questions to uncover what's happening within the business, and not jumping to conclusions based purely on the numbers.

After reviewing your account statements and asking clarifying questions, the bank can then decide whether the run of the account is a strength or weakness.

The operation of your account can have a big impact on the overall assessment, especially if your bank bases its assessment on a credit scoring model, which we will look at later. So, get the operation of your account in order if you're planning to approach the bank in the near future!

What Is Your Level of Commitment?

A Manager can usually get a feel for a person's commitment to a project or a business in a variety of ways. For example, it can come across in their language and the passion with which they talk about the business. The bank wants to see someone who is both passionate and enthusiastic about the project, so you can see now why it's important to look and sound confident.

A business owner's commitment can also be measured in more tangible ways such as how much of their own money is being put into the venture or alternatively how much they have withdrawn from the business over the years. If the owner has regularly injected cash into the business to help with working capital or to purchase new machinery, then this is an encouraging sign. However, if for no apparent reason cash is being withdrawn on a regular basis, then the Manager will have to ask why, as it may not demonstrate full commitment to the business.

But what if only a small amount of cash or no cash at all is being put into a new project? This may not go in your favour. You are asking the bank to put its money at risk so you have to be prepared to put your money at risk as well. If you haven't got any cash all is not lost. Commitment can be evidenced by the fact you may be willing to pledge your house as security, for example.

In the meantime, a question to ask yourself is how does your commitment stack up?

Can You Be Considered a Person of Integrity and Honesty?

This is a difficult one to assess but we all pick up vibes about individuals within a few minutes of meeting them. Things either ring true with you or they don't. Refer back to the earlier section where we looked at your interview preparation and the steps you can take to come across as a good risk. These are the points the Manager will take into consideration.

To back up his intuition the Manager can often get information about someone from other people. Staff within the bank are sometimes a good source of information for Managers. Every office has someone who seems to know everything about people in the locality! These people are a fountain of knowledge.

A Manager invariably moves on to a new branch every few years and so he may not know someone's full background. A Manager will usually ask staff what they know about you - even if you're not a customer.

I was once asked to take on a business from another bank. I asked the staff if they knew of him and boy, did they! It seems that before setting himself up in business, five years earlier he had worked with a local company but was sacked for fraudulently signing cheques drawn on his employer's account and paying himself! He had then started in business on his own and despite everything else checking out, profitable trading, good account with the other bank etc. he was soon shown the door!

If you have skeletons in the cupboard, don't assume they won't come out! If they're bad enough they are bound to surface and it can negatively impact on your chances of success.

What Are The Impressions From Visiting Your Business?

One good way to help the Manager assess your character is to ask her to visit your business premises. If you operate a manufacturing business, or a business that is generally interesting to see, then inviting her around will help her get a better understanding of the business and how it works. Not only will this give her an impression of how you operate but it will also bring your business to life.

Obviously, if you operate from home, as an increasing number of people do, a visit is not going to add much to her assessment but at least it will help her visualise how you operate. However, banks have to be cost conscious and if you are a very small business wanting to borrow £500, you're unlikely to warrant a visit! With lower value requests now being done via an online application the issue of a visit will not arise!

You can very quickly build up an impression of how a business is doing just by walking around. I've been to many businesses where people are frantically running around, staff are in the office with their heads down, customers are coming and going and the phone is constantly ringing in the background. All of this gives the impression of a busy place and perhaps an air of efficiency, which cannot be gained from studying a set of Financial Statements!

On the other hand, I've visited businesses that have an air of depression about them; there doesn't seem to be a "buzz" in the air; the premises are drab and dull. I'd put myself in their customers' shoes and ask what impression I would get if I came in here for the first time.

A visit allows the Manager to get a grip on the business that is lurking behind all the facts and figures. I have also found that an entrepreneur will talk more openly about his business when he's in his own place; he's more relaxed and more willing to share both successes and failures. Most business people enjoy talking about their "baby" and they like nothing more than taking people on a tour of their empire. Walking around premises in this way will prompt questions that the Manager would never have thought of in the office and all of this means he will have a better understanding of how your business works.

Once he's back in the office, everything he has seen helps in building an image of the type of person you are - whether you are an asset or a liability to the business!

CAMPARI – ABILITY

Having the ability to run a business is the difference between success and failure, so it's important for the bank to feel comfortable with your ability - the stronger the better.

Let's consider the areas the bank can look at to help it assess how strong, or otherwise, your ability is.

What Qualifications Do You Have?

In the 'about me' section of your Business Plan you will have listed your qualifications. You may wonder why educational qualifications are important. They mainly demonstrate that you have the commitment to follow things through; obtaining qualifications entails planning and organisational skills, all essential if you are to run a business. If you are already in business, and your education years are already well past, you may feel your qualifications will be of little use in today's environment. However, you can attend various courses, run by local colleges or via home study, to keep your skills up to date, so if you have gone down this route, details of these should be included in your biography.

Your local Business Link or Chamber of Commerce often run courses on starting up in business or various aspects of running a business. If you have attended such courses or seminars, they are worth mentioning.

If your qualifications or the courses you have attended are relevant to your business then this will be classed as a strength. Don't worry if you haven't got a list of successful exam passes as long as your arm. I'm sure you've seen people quoting their qualifications as coming from 'The University of Life' or 'The School of Hard Knocks'. What better qualifications can you have than that? No doubt we all know successful entrepreneurs who haven't got a qualification to their name and dropped out of school as soon as they could and yet went on to run hugely successful businesses!

What Is Your Level of General Business Acumen?

You can usually get a "feel" for someone's aptitude for business from the Business Plan and what comes out in the interview. You soon know whether the person in front of you has "got what it takes" by how he conducts himself, the ideas he has for making a success of the business, and the depth of knowledge about the market he's in.

How to assess business acumen is just as much down to gut feeling as to reviewing your track record in previously running a business, whether it be your own or someone else's. It's up to you how you want to portray your business experience but if you've got a track record make sure you push it.

What Are Your Skills?

Everyone has his or her own skill set when it comes to running a business. It may be a knack for marketing, production, selling or having a flare for the numbers. The Manager's aim is to find your area of expertise and at the same time expose the business' weak areas. If you are strong in marketing but have admitted a lack of aptitude in finance, then you are the weak link in a chain, which has to be corrected.

If you have not tackled your area of weakness, for example by attending a course on financial controls or bringing someone in to do your books, then the bank will see this as further evidence of weakness and so should you. So, before you request to borrow money, review any weak areas, think about how you can tackle them, and then do something about it.

A business owner who has every discipline covered will have a better chance of success than one who doesn't.

Have There Been Past Business Successes or Failures?

Some business people are serial entrepreneurs, starting up new businesses all the time, or selling a successful venture only to go right ahead and start another. Past successes are a reliable guide to future success; the owner has proved himself and has learnt all the tricks of the trade and the things to avoid. A track record like this would be seen as a strength.

On the other hand, a failure in business can be a blot on your copybook. People immediately think this is the end and that they'll never get financial support again. That isn't necessarily the case. As well as learning a lot from having run a previously successful business, you can also learn a great deal from running a business that didn't succeed; you now know the pitfalls and how to avoid the pot holes.

Failure can be the best teacher!

During your interview, you will have been up front about your business experiences, covering both the good and bad. But when you talk about the more colourful periods of your business life, by emphasising past failures and the learning points, you will demonstrate that you have grown and learned from the experience.

These lessons can be a plus point in the assessment process, so don't think it's necessary to gloss over a failed enterprise as that experience could work in your favour!

Sometimes a business can fail due to circumstances outside of your control, and if this is the case then make sure the Manager knows the reasons. It may be that you did everything right and the business was a success until some outside influence or event tripped you up.

The point here is to make sure you have covered all the facts, so the bank can come up with a fair assessment of your business background, what happened and what you have learned.

Is There Evidence of Forward Planning?

One strength that your Manager would like to see is your forward planning ability. Businesses can only be truly successful if they plan ahead. The pace of change in business is such that you need to show you have the ability to think ahead and be up there with the competition. A display of this characteristic will be the fact that you have completed a Business Plan. So many business owners fall down on this point.

If your Plan is comprehensive, including market research, financial forecasts and a detailed marketing strategy, then this will strengthen your case. A lack of any forward thinking will go against you, so demonstrate that you know where you are going.

What Are Your Business Objectives?

In your Business Plan you should have clear objectives for you and your business. These objectives will describe how the business will look in the future in terms of turnover, profitability, number of outlets or shops etc. Your objectives have to be clear and concise, no vague visions or promises.

The bank will review these objectives and consider whether they appear realistic. Are they stretching enough? Do your objectives express clearly enough that you, or your management team, are working to a plan? Is there a clear roadmap? Is there a definition of what success will look like and can the bank and the business measure whether it has been achieved?

It's important for the bank to feel that the business and its owners know where it is heading.

How Strong Are Your Employees' Skills?

It's not only your ability to run a successful business that will be assessed; it's also your employees' skills. They are the ones who are interacting with your customers, producing your products and spending your money! Employees can make or break a business. In your Business Plan you should include an overview of your employees' skill levels. A well skilled and experienced team will be a plus point.

How Suitable Is the Business Location and Premises?

As well as your ability to perform, the bank also needs to consider the business' ability to perform. The business, its set-up, the location and state of the premises are just as important as the management structure and your experience.

In this Internet age, depending on your industry sector, location is now of lesser importance, but for a retail outlet location is of paramount importance. For example, if you are selling highly priced antiques but you are based in a low-income area then you may struggle to succeed.

We have already discussed the benefits of the bank undertaking a visit and one such benefit is the opportunity to review your premises.

A visit gives the bank a chance to assess how the management spend their money! I remember going to visit a start up and seeing the boss sitting behind a desk surrounded by office fittings that cost many thousands of pounds! Yes, it looked great and I'm sure the reasoning was that they had to look the part for prospective customers, but I had the feeling it was more important than anything else. A good yet cheaper set may have been more appropriate for a start up struggling to get on its feet.

Another sign that management are more interested in the trappings of apparent success is the "Porsche" in the car park! I've seen this a few times and whilst it may look good it does put the bank on notice about how the owners see their priorities, especially when you know the business can't afford it! By all means reward your success but ensure it's appropriate and in keeping with the performance of the business.

So take a step back. What does a visitor see when he visits? Does your reception area give an impression of a business on its knees or on the way up? Does your office come across as efficient or one where your staff have to spend 10 minutes looking for that file, which they know "is here somewhere"? Does the décor look tired and so doesn't portray a busy and vibrant business? It's amazing what a lick of paint can do!

Impressions gained do influence the bank when they are assessing a business, so take a long critical look at your premises and do what's needed to create that oh so important first impression.

What Is The Management Structure?

For a one-man business, the structure of the team is pretty clear - it's just you! However, there is an inherent weakness in this; what happens to the business if you fall ill? If you are unable to carry out your duties for 3 months, how are you going to cover your absence?

Who is going to do the selling, the buying or the monthly financials? From the bank's point of view this may put into question how the loan repayment will be made if business was to start slipping away.

When this issue is raised the usual answer from a one-man band is that their husband or wife can cover any periods of absence. Whilst in some businesses that might work this is not practical if the business is in a specialised sector or if the period of absence becomes protracted.

I once remember calling a man to repair a washing machine. Unfortunately he was not taking on any work because he had damaged his ankle ... 3 months before! He couldn't even offer me an alternative name. What was he doing for income? Who knows!

Lack of forward planning in this aspect can be considered a weakness. The only way you can address it is by ensuring you have an insurance policy in place which will provide some income if you become incapacitated for a period of time. This will go some way towards calming the Manager's troubled mind! We will look at the issue of insurance in greater detail later.

If you have plans to employ someone in the near future so they can take over some of your duties, make sure you emphasise this point to the bank. This demonstrates that your business would not be affected in the short term if something happened to you.

If you have a medium to large sized business then the issue of cover in your absence ideally should not arise. It's likely you'll have a separate department for marketing and finance, for example, and so the business should work without you. If it doesn't and you feel you still have to be there all the time, then take a long look as to why your continual presence is still deemed necessary. Do you have too much control? Should you delegate more? A very clear structure with staff responsible for specific roles should leave time for you to concentrate on building up the business, which is what the boss should be doing!

A defined management structure with specific responsibilities will be regarded as a strength.

Is There a Succession or Exit Plan?

So what's your end game plan? It may not seem an important point but it is something that you should be thinking about. If the bank is to give you a long-term loan, they need to be happy that at the end of your day there is someone to take over the business should something happen to you, or a formal exit plan.

Succession is seen as more of an issue in smaller family-run businesses where the children, if there are any, have no interest in taking over. In these cases the bank will want to ensure that any loan or overdraft is paid off well before retirement age.

In a family business, a father grooming his son or daughter to take over the business is seen as a strength because there is an element of continuity and a real reason for the business to succeed. This presupposes, of course, that the children are willing to take on this role and have been trained accordingly. In so many family businesses you hear about children who have rebelled when faced with continuing a legacy they have no interest in.

What is your succession plan?

Is There Ongoing Training?

The bank likes to see a business that has trained and qualified employees. Regular training indicates a firm that takes its future seriously. But training is not only good for the business; it's also good for the motivation and moral of the employees – important in any business.

What on-going training do you give your staff? If the answer is "none", why is that? Training should be an on-going process - there is always something new to learn.

You can see that in assessing your ability the range of issues to cover is vast. Which ones are you strong in and which ones need your urgent attention?

CAMPARI – MARGIN

This part of the CAMPARI framework is nothing to do with a review of the margins you are achieving on sales. The margin being referred to is the interest rate margin the bank will be charging above Base Rate, together with any other lending or arrangement fees. Here, the bank is checking that the price you are being charged and the income it will earn is a fair reward for the risk it is taking.

Like it or not, banks are akin to any other business; they are out to make a profit!

During the credit crunch and its aftermath the issue of bank charges and interest rates has gained a lot of coverage and heightened emotions on both sides. Survey after survey has showed that small business owners have felt taken advantage of as banks arbitrarily raised interest rate margins and fees which on the face of it was done to prop up their falling profits following an increase in bad debts. The anger felt by small businesses was compounded by the fact that many had little option but to accept the position as changing banks was not an option given the tightening in availability of credit.

How the Bank Calculates Your Interest Rate and Arrangement Fees

All banks have a starting price for the money they lend to you; it is called the Base Rate. This is the equivalent of your raw materials or stock cost. To make a profit, you add a margin on to your stock price which adequately reflects the work you have put in to make your product or service saleable. It's the same with your bank. They add a margin on top of their cost of funds (interest paid on customers' deposits which are the bank's equivalent of raw material) and so you will end up being charged one overall figure. However, this is where the similarity ends.

When you sell your product or service, you sell it at one price; the same price to all your customers (unless of course you favour some of your better ones). In most cases, regardless of who the customer is, you charge them the same price.

Yet banks will charge different interest rate margins to different customers. Some businesses will be charged 1% over the Base Rate, while other will be charged 6% over or even higher. Some loans, especially at the lower end of the market, tend to be on fixed rates which stay the same throughout the duration of the loan.

The bank will also charge an arrangement fee for the preparation and underwriting of the deal. The fee can either be a fixed amount (say £250) for a borrowing up to a certain amount, or a percentage based on the amount borrowed, such as a fee ranging from 0.25% up to perhaps 1.5%. As we will see the size of the fee is subject to the same considerations as the calculation of the interest rate margin.

Why does the bank differentiate between customers?

Differing Interest Rates and Fees Are All About Risk

The reason banks apply a different interest rate and fee to different customers is down to its perception of risk – what is the likelihood that they will lose money on you? If you are considered a high risk, there is a bigger likelihood of them losing money and vice versa. To offset any potential loss, they have to make a higher profit and they do this via a larger margin. If you are considered to be a low risk, then you will be charged a lower margin because the bank feels they are less likely to lose money on you.

Whether you are considered a good risk or a poor risk is down to a number of factors. It is an individual assessment. So, what factors does the bank take into consideration when deciding what margin and fee to charge?

Start Ups and Smaller Businesses

For smaller businesses borrowing up to £25,000 or so some banks will go for a set margin over the Base Rate and fixed arrangement fee; a one-size-fits-all approach with little or no room for negotiation. You want the finance? That's what it will cost you ... period. For a start up business the margin and fees will be much higher than for an established business. The reasoning is that the risk in lending to a new business is far higher than lending to a business with a track record.

Established Businesses

If you are a well established business then a different set of criteria will apply.

Your Industry

If you're in a sector which is currently out of favour either with the bank or the economy as a whole, then you can expect a higher margin to be charged. In any cyclical economy there are always industries or sectors which are suffering and companies within these sectors may find themselves paying more to borrow than other businesses. The maxim is, *"The higher the perceived industry risk, the higher the price."*

Your Profitability

If you consistently make good profits then you have a proven track record and this is rewarded with a lower margin and fee. Good long-term profits are an indication that the likelihood of your business failing is lower.

Balance Sheet Strength

During the section on Balance Sheet assessment we looked at a company's Net Worth and saw that this reflects the strength of the business and equates to the reserves, which have been built up over the years. A healthy Net Worth and a low gearing is a positive and can help in achieving a lower overall cost of borrowing.

Length of Time in Business

It's said that up to 60% of new businesses fail within the first three years and so if you are starting out you can expect to pay a larger margin over Base Rate compared to a well-established business. As time goes by, the longer you stay in business the less likely you are to go under; this fact will allow you to negotiate a lower cost.

The Security You Offer

If you are pledging security with a value of twice the loan or overdraft you are asking for, then this will help you negotiate a better deal. I said earlier that pricing depends on how much the bank could lose if you fail. If you bring security which, when sold, will still leave money left over after repaying the bank, then this will be taken into consideration when looking at pricing your loan.

To benefit from lower pricing the security offered would need to be easily valued, and something that can be sold quickly and easily. A guarantee from someone without assets to back it up cannot be considered as first class security and so the facility will be priced as if it were unsecured.

Your Negotiating Skills

We have seen that in some cases you can negotiate a better deal if you have a strong business with a good track record, sound security and the confidence to fight your corner.

Is The Interest Rate and Arrangement Fee an Adequate Reward for the Risk Being Taken?

The bank is going to ask itself whether the interest rate and fee being charged is sufficient reward for the level of risk being taken. If you have an unrealistic expectation of what you are prepared to pay then don't be surprised if the bank walks away. Just as you assess the profitability of a business transaction, so does the bank. The Manager will take a look at the margin and fee being charged and decide if it's a good deal for him or not. If not, then he may be prepared to walk away for fear of setting a precedent, so don't have an unrealistic expectation.

The whole issue of charges has become very emotive over the last few years. Until true competition returns to the market the average sized SME may just have to accept what is being offered in order to secure an offer of finance.

CAMPARI – PURPOSE

The next aspect considered under CAMPARI is the purpose of the loan or overdraft - what is the finance being used for? The bank will be more willing to support a request if the purpose is right both for them and your business.

Let's have a look at the key considerations.

Is It Legal?

Obviously the bank does not want to finance an illegal business! A request to provide an overdraft facility to allow you to purchase drugs which can then be sold for 100% profit with the overdraft being paid off in three weeks won't go very far in the assessment process! Similarly, anything which helps to avoid payment of tax will not be considered a plus point.

Does It Fit With The Bank's Lending Policy?

Banks have business sectors they don't like, and so may not be looking to increase their lending exposure to those sectors. Industries and sectors may be out of favour for a number of reasons:

- In a standard economic cycle, certain sectors may suffer more than others, thereby increasing the lending risk. During the credit crunch banks have been bailing out of supporting pubs and restaurants as they are the first businesses to suffer in a downturn with people reining in their spending habits. The popular buy-to-let market for example, which boomed from early to mid part of the first decade of the 21st century, saw a collapse in funding options as lenders pulled out.

- One bank may already be heavily exposed to a particular sector and so is even more vulnerable if there is a downturn. For example, during the 1980s many UK banks over-extended their loan book to the property sector and when the property bubble burst, they realised too late that they were over-exposed. As a result, the criteria for obtaining a loan in that particular sector was tightened up and so, for a number of years, getting a loan agreed was difficult for all but the very best businesses. Not much different in today's environment I guess! If your bank is over-exposed in your sector, then getting a loan agreed may be hard, unless you have a very strong case.

When assessing your request, the sector you are in will be reviewed and a decision taken as to whether this is a strength or weakness in relation to your request. If the bank's current policy for your sector is a very strongly 'anti', then your request may stop there. Regardless of who you are, as a matter of policy, the answer will be no. Your only options are to either wait for the embargo to be lifted or to seek finance elsewhere. The solution is to ask your Manager before you formally approach the bank as to whether you are 'in or out'.

What Will The Finance Be Used For?

If the funds are to be used for working capital to fund increased sales or to purchase a fixed asset, then you are off to a good start. Banks are more likely to support you if the funds are a 'value add' for your business. Let's say you are looking to buy in a new product line, or invest in additional machinery which will double your production capacity. This is an easy sell and as long as the numbers stack up the case should be clear cut.

But a request to increase your overdraft limit to help pay your VAT bill may be looked at in a different light. Supporting the payment of an urgent creditor is not going to move your business forward. Funding for short term needs does have its place and can be supported, but if requested regularly it's a sign that there is something more fundamentally wrong. There has to be a very clear source of repayment and comfort given that this is not going to be a regular occurrence.

If the requested loan or overdraft is to be used to pay off a debt with another financial institution, then also expect to go through hoops, especially in the current climate. The questions asked will be, "Why is the business looking to repay its debt? Is the other bank demanding its money back? Do they feel uncomfortable with the business' future prospects?"

The answer may simply be that your existing bank is proving to be costly, or the service you are getting is poor. In both cases these reasons are acceptable but it's down to you to clearly demonstrate that you are moving for a business reason (poor service), not a financial reason (you have been turned down and so are looking elsewhere).

Having said that, as we saw earlier, your request may be turned down because your current bankers are not in your sector – your decline was a policy issue. If this is the case then a re-finance would be in order. As ever, it's all about providing an explanation.

Also, remember what I said earlier, the bank is not a venture capitalist or a substitute for risk capital. If your idea is for a new and innovative way of doing something, but it's very experimental and requires money to build a prototype, then bank finance is not for you. If you wish to take your chances by all means have a go but during the assessment process you are unlikely to score very highly.

Can The Purpose Be Proved?

It's not unknown for a business owner to be less than truthful as to why the finance is really needed. Some will ask for a loan to buy a vehicle, for example, and then use the money for another purpose such as paying off other debts. Don't be surprised if the Manager pushes you to produce as much documentary evidence as you can to satisfy himself that the cash will be used for the right reason.

Proof could be in the form of a written quotation or other correspondence, which demonstrates your intent. This is fine if you are buying a capital item such as machinery or vehicles but it's more difficult if you are requesting an overdraft facility for working capital. Of course, anyone can get quotations and at the end of the day, its down to how the Manager views your integrity and honesty - does he believe you?!

Something which may help is a tour around your business. If the Manager can see the business in operation, see where the new machine will go, and understand how it fits in with the rest of the business, then this will go some way to satisfying him and helping him understand that the purpose of the request is a sound one.

Is The Request Correctly Structured - Overdraft or Loan?

Correctly structuring your borrowing is important. A request for help with working capital (to finance debtors, stock and pay creditors) would invariably be financed via an overdraft limit, whereas the purchase of a capital item (machinery or equipment) would be financed by a loan.

Why is this?

If your account has an overdraft limit, the balance of that account should be swinging between credit and debit sometime during a month. All an overdraft is doing is allowing you to pay your creditors and buy in more stock before you collect your debtors. Items paid for from cash, which are not working capital related (day-to-day finance needs) such as vehicles and machinery, suck available liquidity from the business. If you spend £10,000 on a new van, that is £10,000 less you have in the pot to buy stock or fund a new customer via longer credit terms. If you need to finance a piece of equipment, which will be used by the business for, say, 5 years, this would be better placed on a loan or financed via a leasing arrangement.

However, it does not mean that a request for an overdraft to buy a vehicle would not be looked upon favourably. If your cash flow is so positive that the amount borrowed on overdraft can be paid off within a few months, then that's fine; you only need to prove this through your Cash Flow Forecast, which will demonstrate the level of liquidity you have to play with.

Another way to finance the day-to-day requirements of the business is to utilise Invoice Discounting or Factoring. These products, which we looked at earlier, are better suited to medium-sized businesses but they are an alternative to the traditional overdraft.

If your request is not correctly structured then this would be a weakness, but it's something that is easily put right by matching the right product with your need.

Is It The Right Thing To Do For The Business?

There are instances where a business is already borrowing heavily and it may not be in their best interest to borrow additional money. This could be because existing loan repayments or interest costs are already proving to be a strain and borrowing more may not be the right decision. In an economic downturn a business which has borrowed heavily could suffer more than a business which has no or limited borrowing. A fall in profit or a disruption in cash flow could lead to an inability to cover interest costs or loan repayments. Would advancing further money be the right way forward?

Trying to tell someone that they are already borrowing too much and that another loan may not be in their best interest is not easy – the owner is keen to get on with his plans or desperate to pay a pressing creditor and so he usually won't hear the Manager's words of caution. Banks may be accused of stifling entrepreneurs, and that could be the case especially during the last few years, but they are also there to temper your enthusiasm.

If you are faced with this reluctance, listen to what is being said, evaluate it and then make a reasoned decision as to the way forward - do you take his advice or storm out and go elsewhere? Ask what the Manager sees in your business that he doesn't like so you know and understand his areas of concern.

CAMPARI – AMOUNT

We are now coming to the main part of the assessment process - how much you want to borrow. In this part of the framework the Manager will review the amount being requested and decide if it's a request he feels comfortable with, taking into consideration the size of the business, the information gleaned from the Financial Statements and Forecasts and what he has learned from your Business Plan and interview.

Let's look at the considerations surrounding the amount you wish to borrow.

Are You Making a Contribution Towards the Project?

We have already mentioned that banks want to see you investing or risking some of your own money in the venture. Investing in a business is not a one-way street. The bank needs to see that you are tied into or committed to the business by having your own resources at stake. The bank will also be comforted by the fact that the risk within a project has been spread across a number of supporters.

As a rule of thumb, during 'normal' times the bank looked at a minimum injection of 25% to 30% of the project cost. Post-credit crunch it is not unusual for this to now range from 30% to 50% depending on the industry, your track record and security offered. A good stake in any project will go a long way to improving the chances of success.

The source of the cash injection will also be a consideration. If you are borrowing your contribution from another bank or finance company then this will be a negative point against you. The reason for this is that the loan will be an additional finance cost to service and will put a further strain on the business. It's up to you to demonstrate via the Cash Flow Forecasts that all the financing can be comfortably serviced.

However, having said that, not all outside borrowing is regarded as a black mark. If you have raised a mortgage to withdraw available equity on your private property then this is a demonstration of your commitment to the business, i.e. you are prepared to risk your house to help the business succeed. Another example could be a family loan. Loans from parents or other family members are not uncommon and this usually provides an extra incentive to ensure success! Contributions can also come in the form of grants or 'soft' loans, where repayment terms are very flexible.

"For loans of under £50k and above £5k, we often find that getting one lender or a local authority to offer £2,000 or £3,000 has helped a lot in getting other lenders to say yes.

Lenders seem more ready to support if another lender has already agreed to a loan. Somehow it gives them comfort and the chance to say, "Well other people were prepared to lend too" if things go wrong."

Albert Wright, Small Business Solutions Ltd
www.sbsltd.net

If the source of your stake is savings the Manager may ask to see statements of your savings accounts to satisfy himself that the cash really is coming from there.

If you have an existing overdraft limit and you have reduced the outstanding balance over time via retained profits then you can legitimately use the surplus in that facility as your stake. If your average overdrawn balance is £20,000 and you have an overdraft limit of £50,000, you have £30,000 that can be used towards a specific project. All you are doing is utilising past profits or using the Net Worth you have built up over the years. However, make sure you are not using your available working capital, especially if your plan is to expand the business. This is why forward financial planning is so important where new projects are concerned; don't make the mistake of using all your spare cash on start up, leaving nothing left for day-to-day running.

Some business owners try and put a value to the time they have invested in the project and use that as a stake. The bank may look favourably on this if everything else stacks up but with lending criteria having tightened up don't expect miracles!

Will the lack of a cash stake totally scupper your chances? Not necessarily. If the business case is that strong then a stake may be overlooked but with the new lending regime in force, this will only apply to a business with a very long and successful track record. For a start up, a cash stake is now essential.

What Does the Cash Flow Forecast Show?

Your Business Plan will include a Cash Flow Forecast which estimates your peak overdraft requirement. The bank will check that the amount you are requesting ties in with the figure shown in your forecast. It's no good asking for an overdraft limit of £50,000 when your forecast indicates you only need £20,000.

It may not be unreasonable to ask for a small margin on top for contingency purposes. A small leeway may give you the necessary breathing space to sort out problems without having the bank on your back. However, a figure significantly out of line with your forecasts will indicate that you pay scant regard to what your forecasts tell you. Be sensible in what you ask for.

Is The Right Amount Being Requested?

Many business owners don't like to borrow; they have it in their psyche that it's wrong to borrow. When they realise that it's necessary to have support from the bank they try to borrow as little as they can. Their Cash Flow Forecast may indicate they need an overdraft facility of £100,000 but they say they only feel comfortable with £20,000 and stick with this.

What happens? The business achieves the level of turnover it was projecting (perhaps higher) and so larger amounts of cash are needed to fund a growing list of debtors and a bigger stock holding. With an inadequate overdraft limit, the account soon comes under pressure and the small limit is breached time and time again. The result is an unnecessarily tarnished track record with the bank all because the business owner tried to be too conservative.

The moral of the story is that asking for a smaller amount than you really need could ultimately take up more of your time in seeking a higher limit (one that you should have asked for in the first place) and damage your track record with the bank through the regular breaches of your overdraft limit. This doesn't say a lot about your planning ability or financial acumen.

Sometimes though it is the bank that can force you into having an overdraft limit or loan that's smaller than you actually need; essentially, the bank likes your business but it doesn't feel comfortable going to the debt level you are asking for, so they slim down the amount they are prepared to fund. This can work out in one of two ways:

- You accept the lower funding and embark on the project. However, without the full amount you need you are setting yourself up for failure. If at all possible avoid taking a lower amount than you need.

- The flip side to this is that a lower level of finance can enforce a good sense of financial discipline. If you get near your overdraft limit you speed up your debtor collection, you delay paying your creditors, and you look for ways of being more financially efficient. If you have too much headroom in your funding facility the chances are you will become lazy and lax in handling your finances.

Does the Amount Requested Look Right?

Common sense comes into play here. If a bank receives a request from an established business to lend £60,000, but on average all that is being paid into the account each month ranges from £500 to £1,000, then the amount requested looks out of line in relation to the size of the business!

At the end of the day your Business Plan has to clearly demonstrate very good reasons as to why your business needs the amounts you are requesting. Don't just pluck a figure out of the air. If your reasoning is vague or you can't back up your request with evidence then you will have a difficult task convincing a bank to support you.

LOAN SHARP

CAMPARI – REPAYMENT

No bank is going to lend to any business unless it can see exactly how the debt will be repaid. In this part of the assessment process the Manager reviews your financial forecasts. The forecasts are the primary source of information which demonstrates that the finance you are requesting can be paid back. Given the financial climate the whole issue of serviceability has taken on even greater importance.

In preparing your Business Plan and projections you should prepare two or three different versions based on a number of 'what if' scenarios. The key assumptions to play with would be increasing the interest rate you'd be charged by an additional 3% to 4% (Base Rates will increase over time) and flexing the assumed sales growth downwards. This 'stress' testing should show how resilient your business would be to changes in the external environment.

When reviewing the financial forecasts what are the issues being examined?

Has Your Ability To Repay Been Demonstrated?

The lessons learned over the last few years have placed a greater burden on business owners to prove that the amount borrowed can be repaid. As a result you are now much more likely to be asked to produce your forecasts and then have them reviewed, analysed and generally pulled apart. The key points to remember are:

- If you have requested a loan with a monthly repayment your forecasts should show that you can afford to comfortably meet the commitment;
- If you have requested an overdraft limit your forecast must show that you can cover the interest.

One point to be aware of about Cash Flow Forecasts in particular and overdraft limits is that you don't have to show that you will be repaying it within 12 months; it's not unreasonable to have an overdraft limit in place for a number of years. Remember that the limit is financing your turnover and as long as you are making sales, you may need your limit.

It's human nature to be overly optimistic at times, especially when asking for money, and so neither your Cash Flow nor Profit and Loss Forecast will be taken at face value. To safeguard against an over-zealous entrepreneur, the bank will spend time taking the forecasts apart and testing the assumptions behind the figures.

Questions to Consider When Reviewing Your Profit And Loss and Cash Flow Forecasts

- Does the projected increase in sales look realistic? If there is a large hike in sales has this been adequately explained?
- On what basis are sales going to increase? Has an improvement or deterioration in the general economic scene been taken into consideration?
- Have stock requirements been accurately assessed? On what basis have the requirements been worked out?
- Is the business dependent on materials or stock being delivered on time? If so, how has that risk been addressed in cash flow terms?
- If sales are projected to increase have costs been

reviewed upward?

- If new borrowing has been requested, have the loan repayments and interest charges been included?
- What interest rate has been assumed in the cost of finance calculations?
- Does it look as if all overheads have been included?
- Are the monthly opening and closing balances correct and do all the figures add up? (It's surprising how often this is not the case!)
- Have alternative forecasts been prepared based on various 'what if' scenarios?
- What terms of credit have been used? Are they similar to the previous year? If not, why not?
- As the Cash Flow Forecast will only show the estimated balance at the end of the month is there likely to be a higher peak during the middle of the month?
- Does the Cash Flow Forecast show all proposed capital expenditure, new loans agreed and any money introduced by the owners?

The overriding consideration is whether the forecasts look reasonable, are they consistent with what the business owner has told the bank and, if the business is already established, how do the forecasts compare with performance to date. If there are any areas which require clarification then expect to be called in again so the issues can be resolved.

What Is Your Previous Repayment Track Record Like?

Although the subject of how your bank account operates was considered under the Character aspect of CAMPARI, it is also a valid part of the Repayment assessment. If you have been banking with the same bank for some time and have had previous loans then your repayment track record will be reviewed and taken into consideration. The same applies to any overdraft limits you may have had; have the limits been respected?

I mentioned earlier that if you bank elsewhere, the Manager would request copies of your statements and ask similar questions – what is your financial track record like? The way you have operated your account in the past is a good indication of your ability to repay in the future. If you struggled to keep up with your last loan repayments, or you constantly exceeded your limit, this says a lot about your character – are you financially trustworthy?

Is The Repayment Term Acceptable?

In asking for a loan to purchase, for example, a vehicle, the loan repayment period has to tie in with its life expectancy. It's no good purchasing a vehicle that is expected to last for 4 years and yet request a loan repayable over 10 years. By the time you need a new vehicle you will still be paying for the old one! The repayment period has to tie in with the expected life of the asset being bought. The only exception to this is buying a building which can be repaid over a 20 or 25 year period.

Is There A Secondary Source Of Repayment?

Bankers are a pessimistic bunch - they will look for a secondary source of repayment, or a 'get out of jail' card! The question they will ask is, "What is the alternative way out for the bank if the business collapses and some of the debt remains outstanding?"

You would not be expected to cover this in your Business Plan - explaining how the bank can get its money back if the business goes belly-up will not come across as a positive statement! However, it's a question worth thinking about. How would you answer it?

The answer to this question is usually the value of the security being offered and we will consider this in more depth later.

Your Personal Income and Expenditure, Assets and Liabilities

I have said previously that for a small business the bank is looking to you as the person who will ensure the debt is repaid; they are lending to you as an individual, not to the business. The bank will therefore want to know what your personal financial situation is. They may ask you to complete a personal Income and Expenditure Statement, which will detail your in-goings and outgoings. Ideally this should show a surplus each month.

They may also wish to know the extent of your personal assets and liabilities (personal debts). Whilst not strictly related to your business you could refuse to provide the information but the more open you are the better understanding the bank has of whom it's dealing with.

What Do The Financial Statements Reveal?

We have already examined the key points the bank will look for when reviewing a set of Accounts; past profitability, strength of the Balance Sheet, the key ratios, all will be considered and then an overall assessment given as to whether the Accounts are a strength or weakness. As you will know, when you invest in any financial product there is always a health warning which says, 'past performance is not a guarantee to future performance'. The same applies to Financial Statements!

Whilst your Accounts may show exceptional or even poor performance, it doesn't mean this will happen again in the future. Your Business Plan, and the reason for your request, may be aimed at putting right your poor performance or even capitalising on your past successes but the bank still needs to consider past performance because it's a representation of how you manage your business.

If you are a start up then obviously you will not have Financial Statements and so to prove that you can service your interest or loan repayment the bank will concentrate purely on your forecasts and the other information you have provided.

What Do The Management Accounts Reveal?

When reviewing Financial Statements I mentioned that one disadvantage of relying on them is that the information is out of date. On average, it can take 6 to 9 months for a business to have its accounts prepared and a lot can happen in that time. To overcome this disadvantage the bank may ask for more up to date information in the form of Management Accounts.

If you keep monthly or quarterly trading figures you have up to date information on performance and as a result you can spot and quickly respond to any potential problems. For any business, just relying on the annual Financial Statements to see if they are making a profit is not an ideal situation.

If monthly or quarterly figures are produced then they will be analysed in the same way as annual figures with trends being assessed and a view taken on overall performance.

CAMPARI – INSURANCE

In the final part of the assessment process, 'insurance' is taken in a much wider context than the question, "Is the business or individual insured?" Insurance addresses the problem of what the bank looks to for repayment if the lending doesn't work out i.e. what security is being offered.

What Security Is Available or Being Offered?

For most business owners, the issue of interest rates, charges and security are the points of tension when negotiating a finance facility. But of all these contentious points, security is by far the most emotive.

The owner's argument is that the business should stand on its own two feet and does not need security to back it up, especially if it has been demonstrated that the business will have no problem in servicing the debt. In theory this is fine but banks have to admit that no matter how good their credit assessment is, there are always going to be businesses that fail ... this has been clearly seen in the aftermath of the credit crunch and economic downturn.

If, after closure of the business and disposal of business assets, there is clearly no hope of getting repaid in full, then the bank needs a fall back position to cover the shortfall and this is where security comes in.

Banks, as we have seen, are more concerned with serviceability; they don't want to sell a business premises or someone's home if they can help it. Security is merely a back up if all else fails.

Security Criteria

Banks will not take just any assets as security. For the security to be deemed acceptable it has to satisfy three criteria:

- Easy to value – a value has to be attached to the asset. If it's difficult to value then this brings into question how easy it would be to realise the asset in a sale.
- Easy to take a legal charge or mortgage over – there has to be a way of the bank staking a legally recognised 'claim' against the asset. Being named as an interested party means the asset cannot be disposed of without the bank's knowledge.
- Easy to liquidate – the asset has to have a ready market so it can be sold as quickly as possible.

You must remember though that banks will not lend solely against security as a pawnbroker does. A pawnbroker has customers coming to him bringing an item against which he lends an appropriate amount. He does not concern himself with serviceability of the loan and whether the owner can afford to repay; he has the security to more than cover the debt. From the banker's perspective it's serviceability first and security second. Security is a protection or an insurance policy and not the main reason for agreeing to lend money.

What does the bank consider as acceptable security?

Land and Buildings

This is one of the most common forms of security offered. The Title Deeds can either be in the name of the business, the personal name of the owner or even an unconnected 3rd party. Most owners have no problem in pledging business assets but it's a different ball game when it comes to pledging personal assets such as a home. This can be a very contentious issue.

The bank will look upon a house being given as security as a sign of commitment. You may look at it differently - it's the family home and should not be risked under any circumstances. If the business is very well established and has a good trading record then the bank will usually rely on business assets to support the borrowing but for younger enterprises, where the risk of failure is higher, you may be fighting a losing battle.

To establish the value the bank will instruct a professional valuer to review the property. They will give two values:

- An open market value which is the figure likely to be achieved if sufficient time is given to sell;
- A forced sale value, which is a figure likely to be achieved if a sale has to be achieved within a short timescale.

Debenture

A Limited Company is a separate legal entity from its directors and shareholders and so all the assets belong to it and can be pledged to support any borrowing. Assets such as land can be taken as security but the company still has other assets which have a value, for example, plant and machinery, debtors and stock. All of these have an inherent value and can be pledged to the bank.

A Debenture creates a fixed and floating charge over the assets:

- Fixed charge. This will cover:
  - ❑ land (although this is usually legally charged separately, an "interest" can still be registered via a Debenture)

- plant and machinery which is physically fixed to the floor or building
- Floating charge. This will cover:
  - debtors
  - stock - raw materials; work in progress and finished goods
  - plant and machinery not fixed, for example, smaller machines, tools and general furniture
  - cash

Business owners often argue that taking a Debenture will provide the Bank with all the security it needs; after all, "The debtors and stock amount to £100,000 and all I need is £50,000, so the bank is more than covered. You don't need my house, factory or personal guarantee."

You are right up to a point but the rationale of having debtors and stock covering your borrowings only applies when the business is successful. Banks will not be looking to realise its security when all is going well; it only needs to take action when things have gone wrong. In a distressed situation such as this, the assets under a Debenture rarely fetch as much as was available when it was initially taken. When a disposal takes place the vultures swoop and values hit rock bottom.

Why a Debenture Never Realises What You Think It's Worth

When a business is going downhill and losing money, this is what happens:

- Cash becomes short because the business is not as profitable as it once was

- Debtors are collected as quickly as possible and because business is declining, the debtor book shrinks each month
- Stock levels are wound down and not replaced in order to release much needed cash
- The cash that is available is used up; machinery and equipment are sold

The result is that by the time the business has finally folded, or the bank realises that something is wrong, all the assets that could quickly be turned into cash (debtors and stock) have gone, or substantially reduced, leaving very little under the Debenture for the bank to realise.

Experience shows that even if anything is left, it rarely achieves its true value when sold. If there are uncollected debtors they will be the ones that proved difficult to collect when the company was still trading because the debtor either couldn't pay or there was a dispute with the underlying contract. As a result, the collection rate can sometimes be as low as 40%, or even lower, of the face value of the remaining debtor book.

Similarly, stock never achieves its true value in a distressed sale - how many bankruptcy auctions have you been to and picked up a bargain? As soon as an item is known to be from a business which is no longer trading you can knock 50% to 70% off its true value, depending on what is being sold and which industry it's from.

Until recently banks felt safe in the knowledge that at least any money due to the company was caught under the fixed charge element of the Debenture and this meant that no other creditor could have a prior claim. This was thrown into doubt following a case ruling in New Zealand, referred to as 'Brumark'.

In the ruling the Judge decided that a charge over debtors could only be floating and this meant that any claims from preferential creditors (mainly Government bodies such as PAYE and VAT) would rank ahead of the bank in terms of the debtor funds.

A test case was brought in the UK with Nat West v. Spectrum (2005) which confirmed the ruling. However, the effect of it was reduced following the passing of The Enterprise Act in 2003 which abolished the Crown's preferential status, leaving very few recognised creditors that can rank in front of the bank (these creditors will comprise of the costs of the administration and employee claims).

What does this mean for you if you run a Limited Company? It means that the available pot of money that banks could look to as part of a company's asset base and so its security are now depleted. The implication for directors and shareholders is that banks are even more likely to look to other security to bolster their position, which will be either land and buildings or personal guarantees. One way round this is that banks can finance debtors through factoring or invoice discounting which does not get caught up in this ruling. This reduces any overdraft requirement.

Banks knows through bitter experience that security rarely fetches what they originally thought, so don't try and argue that there are sufficient assets to cover your borrowing; it may be the case now, when all is going swimmingly well, but it won't be when the bank needs the assets most.

Personal or Directors' Guarantees

If you are a sole trader, or in partnership, then you are personally responsible for your debts and that of the business. However, if you

operate through a Limited Company it is a separate legal entity and is solely responsible for its debts.

As you will have learned so far, one of the key areas the bank likes to see is evidence of commitment and if the bank is lending to a limited company, it will always ask the directors to enter into a personal guarantee.

Basically a guarantee is a written promise by a third party stating that if the company defaults he or she will personally meet the liability. Guarantees from company directors are commonplace and are requested as a matter of course in addition to Debentures and any legal charge over land and buildings, more so now following the Brumark ruling.

As security, guarantees can be little more than a sign of good faith, especially if the bank knows that the guarantor (the person giving the guarantee) has little in the way of personal assets. If the guarantor does own a house he may be asked to pledge it to support his guarantee. If the bank calls upon the guarantee it can then look to the property to fulfil the guarantee commitment.

"From a legal viewpoint if you are asked to provide a personal guarantee:-

(1) Read what you are being asked to sign and then read it again!

Ensure you read all the paperwork that needs to be signed and make a note of sections you need clarifying. Don't be in a rush to sign anything put before you, there are often 'hidden' capture clauses in the documents giving very wide ranging rights in favour of the other party.

(2) Take independent legal advice before signing

Ensure you take full advantage of that advice by preparing beforehand to ensure that you get the answers to your questions. You can access free advice from many

High Street firms but it pays to get some paid for advice addressing the whole document and any questions you may have.

(3) Remind yourself what you have done

Don't enter into a guarantee and forget about it. Not a problem perhaps unless there's a downward turn in your finances. Review your guarantees on a regular basis.

Guarantees often allow the person providing the guarantee (if with some effort and business ramifications) to terminate their guarantee. If you are aware of the situation you can at least take financial and legal advice before the worst happens to explore the option of terminating the guarantee early. A guarantee which does not allow termination may be challenged in some circumstances."

Stephanie Barber, Retired Solicitor at Lime One Ltd, www.limeone.co.uk

Guarantees can either be unlimited, which means that there is no limit to the amount of the guarantee, or limited whereby the guarantor's liability is limited to a sum specified within the documentation. Providing a personal guarantee can be an emotive issue and after a period of time many directors will attempt to have the guarantee requirement removed. The arguments used are that a successful track record has been established via a trouble-free account performance and a consistent profit record. Whether you are successful in such a request depends on how much leverage you have with the bank. In all but long associations and exceptional amounts of security being held, the request would usually be resisted.

Stocks and Shares

Share certificates for publicly quoted companies can be taken as security but they are not ideal because obviously the value can fluctuate, as has been seen over recent years. However, if deposited, they can be taken as a sign of faith but because of the possible fluctuations in the value, only 50% to 75% of the current value will be taken into account when calculating the overall value available to cover the borrowing.

Life Policies

Individuals take out life policies so that in the event of death a lump sum is paid out to their estate or a named beneficiary. From a business' point of view this provision can be useful if a policy is taken out with the aim of helping the business if one of the key players dies. For example, if a business is run by two people and one of them dies this could leave too large a gap for the remaining partner to fill, so placing additional and unwanted pressure on him or her. Such pressure could conceivably put the future of the business at risk. The pay out on a life policy specifically taken to cover a loan would be used to pay off the borrowing thereby relieving the remaining partner of any financial stress during a time when the business may struggle.

"The loss of a partner or director may destabilise a business and can quickly lead to financial difficulties. Partner/Director Share Protection means if the worst does happen the remaining directors or partners can stay in control of the business. In the event of a partner or director dying or falling terminally or critically ill, Partner/Director Share Protection can provide a sum of money to the remaining partner(s) or director(s). This means that in the event of a valid claim the policy could pay out an amount sufficient to purchase the deceased or critically ill

partner's/director's interest in the business.

The loss of the person or people who have guaranteed a loan is particularly serious for a business. Business Loan Protection helps you pay an outstanding overdraft, loan or commercial mortgage, should the guarantor die or become terminally or critically ill.

Key Person Protection helps safeguard a business against the financial effects of death, terminal illness, or critical illness of a key person. The loss of a key person may result in reduced sales, loss of profit/turnover, wasted time, recruitment costs, and disruption of development plans or increased workloads for remaining staff."

Chris Price, Chris Price Financial Consultancy, www.financialconsultancy.org.uk

If the bank sees that the successful operation of a business depends upon both of the directors or partners, then it may take any available life polices as security or insist that a new policy is taken out. By taking the policies as formal security, in the event of death, the proceeds will automatically go to the bank, not the deceased's estate, and then used to reduce or repay any borrowings.

In the case of sole traders, having a life policy as security can be equally important. A sole trader business by its very nature relies on one person to run it or provide direction. If he or she dies then the business effectively dies as well, leaving the family to deal with any debts. The bank would not want to be exposed in this way and so having a life policy as security will avoid any potential risk and also makes sense for the owner's family.

Unsecured Borrowings

Some businesses do have overdrafts or loans where they have not provided any security. Under what circumstances can this happen?

- There may be a very long association with the bank, such that a respectable track record has been built up and the chance of the bank losing money is remote.
- A very large stake has been put in. The level of commitment demonstrated is such that security is not really an issue.
- The amount borrowed is so small that it is not worth the effort or cost of the bank taking any security. Also, if they had to rely on that security by selling a house, for example, to cover a debt of £10,000, the bad publicity and legal costs simply would not justify it.

Enterprise Finance Guarantee (EFG)

In January 2009, in response to an almost complete shutdown in bank lending to SMEs, the government launched the Enterprise Finance Guarantee. The scheme provides a guarantee to participating banks to allow them to support businesses that have a viable business or start up plan but lack the security the bank would normally look for.

The government guarantees up to 75% of the bank's exposure and in return for the guarantee the bank (and ultimately the borrower) is charged a 2% premium per annum on the outstanding balance, assessed and paid quarterly. The scheme was originally to run to March 2010 but has since been extended to March 2011.

Banks came under some criticism during the early days of the scheme for not actively making it available or incorrectly understanding it. Reports of businesses being declined finance but not told about the EFG scheme were commonplace. However, there does now appear to be a better take up but still little appreciation amongst SMEs as to the benefits.

Features of the Enterprise Finance Guarantee Scheme

- The government provides a guarantee to the bank of 75% of the outstanding loan balance
- The decision to lend lies with the bank; the government has no part in the credit assessment process
- Loan terms on a commercial basis i.e. no preferential treatment
- The guarantee covers loans from £1,000 to £1 million. The starting level is discretionary and may be pegged at higher amounts by some banks
- Available for businesses with a turnover of up to £25 million
- Premium of 2% per annum payable quarterly and based on the outstanding balance
- The bank can take an unsupported personal guarantee from company directors for the full value of the loan
- Types of facilities covered:
  - New loans
  - Refinancing of current loans if it can be shown that the business cannot meet the payments or where a deteriorating value of the security could lead to the loan being called in
  - Short-term overdrafts
  - Refinancing of overdrafts to loans to release new working capital
  - Invoice financing facilities

If you are approaching a bank for finance and security is the key weakness in your plan make sure your bank discusses this option with you. If you are not told about the scheme by your bank, then ask! Most industry sectors are covered so call your bank to check your eligibility. For a list of participating banks go to this link: **www. berr.gov.uk/whatwedo/enterprise/finace/efg/page50162.html**

Does the Security Fit the Bank's Criteria?

We have now considered all types of security that are available for the bank to take. In assessing whether the security provided is a strength or weakness, the bank will look at what is offered and see if it fits its ideal security characteristics being:

- Easy to value
- Easy to take a legal charge or mortgage over
- Easy to liquidate if the business fails to pay

As part of the CAMPARI mnemonic, it is appropriate that security, or "Insurance", comes at the end of the assessment process, because that is how it is viewed – security is realised or sold at the very end, after all possibilities have been explored, and only as the last resort. Banks, as I mentioned, are not pawnbrokers, they will not lend money purely against a set of Title Deeds; serviceability, being the ability to cover overdraft interest or loan repayments, is the key. The security taken is the protection if things don't go to plan. In pledging assets, whether personal or business, you must understand that security can and does get realised or sold off to pay borrowings which businesses have failed to pay. Don't think that it will never happen, it can and it does. In offering assets as security, only pledge them on the understanding that the possibility that you may lose them is very real. If you do fall into trouble there's no point pleading to the bank not to sell up; you are unlikely to get very far. The message is that you should pledge your assets with your eyes open.

SWOT ANALYSIS

We have looked at each of the key areas in assessing a request to borrow money. CAMPARI is a very useful tool for Managers to be guided by and ensures that all the key points of your request are reviewed. The main purpose of CAMPARI is to stimulate debate and discussion, either during the Manager's self assessment while reviewing the request, or with his superiors if your request has to be referred to a higher authority.

Let's now move on to another useful assessment tool, which complements CAMPARI, the SWOT analysis framework.

We have indirectly started to look at the SWOT analysis by seeing that you can review each element of CAMPARI and rate the findings as either a strength or weakness. You can see how SWOT adds another dimension to the assessment process.

"In or out of a Business Plan, a SWOT analysis can be a really useful tool. It is not a bad thing to have a bigger list of Weaknesses and Threats than Strengths or Opportunities.

Apart from the benefits of being aware of the things that might damage your business, almost every Weakness represents an Opportunity, it may be that you can learn the skill or buy the equipment to overcome it – look at Gap clothing moving into Gap Kids or McDonalds doing salads.

Continuing with the burger theme, if you were a burger bar threatened by the opening of a large franchise you could use personal service and flexibility as selling tools. Equally some things that you have as strengths may also be weaknesses - strong in a certain age group could also be a weakness because you are only strong in that age group.

The point here is that doing a SWOT analysis can really start you thinking about what you are doing and why."

Chris Olchawski AIBC, Tutsan Associates
www.tutsanuk.com

Strengths and Weaknesses

The Strengths and Weaknesses analysis is useful in crystallising the thoughts process as regards the strength or otherwise of the loan request being made. Strengths and weaknesses are internal factors affecting the business which can be controlled or influenced by the management of the company.

In our review of how the bank analyses Financial Statements, you will recall that all aspects of the Profit and Loss and Balance Sheet can be assessed as a strength or weakness. Is the liquidity ratio a strength or weakness? Is the underlying trend seen over the years a cause for concern or is it one of the business' key strengths?

Moving onto CAMPARI, we have seen that all of the questions and issues raised can be categorised as a strength or weakness. Is the age or health of the owner a strength or weakness? Does your Cash Flow Forecast demonstrate that the business, in all likelihood, can repay the loan (strength) or are there too many overly optimistic assumptions which make repayment doubtful (weakness)?

Being able to look at the request from the perspective of strengths and weaknesses can be a powerful tool and help bring order to what could be a large amount of information.

Opportunities and Threats

Opportunities and Threats are events which are outside your sphere of influence. In other words, you have no say or control over whether the event happens or not; you just have to deal with it or ignore it. However, these events may have a direct impact on your business - both good and bad - so the bank needs to take these into consideration when assessing your request.

These opportunities or threats can be wide and varied and you'll be surprised to see what they are once you sit down to think about it. Whether a certain event is an opportunity or a threat depends upon which industry is being assessed - one industry's opportunity is another one's threat. So, when assessing a request, the Manager has to decide what opportunities and threats your business faces and ultimately take a balanced view as to the likely impact - will it be negative or positive?

One way of helping in the assessment of outside risk is to use the LEPEST framework:

Legal; Environmental; Political; Economic; Sociological; Technological

These areas cover the issues businesses have to deal with either regularly or periodically.

Legal Issues

Is the business in a sector which could be subject to legal problems or is it in a position to take advantage of new or impending legislation? Take the issue of the ban on smoking in pubs and other public places.

Pubs have certainly suffered due to this legislative change.

Environmental Issues

Increasingly, businesses are finding that they have to comply with new health and safety regulations on an almost daily basis, it seems. Heavy fines, or even threats of imprisonment, usually accompany these new regulations and so the risk is very real.

Political Issues

Is your business in a sector which is supported or favoured by the current government but is known to be at odds with the other political parties? What would be the impact if the political climate changed? Would a change represent an opportunity or a threat?

Economic Issues

No business can have control or influence over a country's economy yet it has the greatest impact on them. The recent recession and its impact on businesses has clearly demonstrated how vulnerable some businesses can be to outside events. Was your business in a sector which was heavily hit? Perhaps you are a debt collector, an industry which grows in times of economic pressure!

What about future interest rates? If the market is predicting a large increase in interest rates over the next few years, how will this affect your business? This is particularly relevant if your business is highly borrowed.

If you are an importer or exporter, what is the exchange rate outlook for the major currencies you deal in? Will a shift in rates have a beneficial or negative impact on your business? Opportunity or threat?

How about changes in taxation made during the annual Budget? These only have an impact on businesses which are directly affected by changes in tariffs or taxes but in assessing the business, the impact has to be considered. A wines and spirits retailer faces this problem every year. If duties have been increased then this is a threat to the business but if they have been reduced (is this ever likely to happen?) it could be seen as an opportunity.

What's the impact of inflation on your business? Do you produce products which are a discretionary spend and so in times of high inflation would be priced out of the market?

Sociological Issues

Society and its needs are constantly changing. Our lifestyle and the way we live are constantly moving. Our values and beliefs as a society do shift over time. The bank needs to assess whether your business is threatened by these shifts or is in a position to take advantage.

Take the producers of mineral water; they have seen a huge jump in demand over the years because of the shift away from drinking tap water. Anyone assessing the impact of social changes would say that this is an opportunity for businesses in this sector.

In rural areas the impact of out of town developments, or the opening of a large supermarket in the locality, can have catastrophic effects on small retailers.

What about the changing demographics in our society? We are living longer and are more active in retirement years. Does your business have an opportunity to take? You certainly would if you specialise in holidays for retired people, or health care.

Technological Issues

Technological advancements are moving so fast that it is difficult to decide whether any business can get away with not being affected at all. However, some are more vulnerable than others and some will stand to gain more than others.

Builders, for example, have little to fear from technological advances. There will always be a demand for houses and repairs. However, if you are a traditional retailer in books and CDs, the rapid expansion in online retailing can be seen as a threat. If you are starting out in retailing online, then technological advances and the growing ease with which people are buying online, is definitely seen as an opportunity.

The SWOT and LEPEST analysis frameworks are useful tools to help bring order to the information contained in your Business Plan and gleaned from the interview, and also to prompt further questions to be asked or issues clarified.

As we will see in the next chapter, once all the information is pulled together it makes the decision-making process easier and hopefully the answer – a yes or a no – should be that much clearer.

WHAT YOU HAVE BEEN WAITING FOR – THE DECISION!

After reviewing the CAMPARI and SWOT / LEPEST framework you now have a clear understanding of the areas which a Manager would review in considering your request for finance.

The main benefit of raising issues via use of the frameworks is that it gives the Manager an overview of all aspects of the business; it allows him to make an objective decision by taking all the factors into consideration. It avoids a 'gut feeling' assessment which has been arrived at without taking into account all the facts.

By the end of the thinking, pondering and review process, the final decision as to whether the request should be granted or submitted for approval is simple - the Manager will "know", from reviewing the facts, by looking at the strengths, weaknesses, opportunities and threats, whether on balance you and your business can pay back the money.

It can be argued that the Manager is still relying on "gut feeling" because many of the assessment factors contained within CAMPARI, SWOT and LEPEST are based on perception and not necessarily fact. There is an element of truth in this but from his experience, he will be able to sense whether the business has a chance of success. However, at the end of the day the information gathered during the assessment process will assist in backing up his decision with as many facts as possible.

Referring Your Request for Approval

There are three ways an application can be reviewed.

Credit Scoring

For amounts ranging anywhere between £1 and £20,000 (this varies from bank to bank) your application may be credit scored. Your application is keyed into the bank's lending system and then, against a set criteria, is automatically assessed and given a mark or rating. The rating given to each component is based on the bank's past experience – did businesses displaying a certain rating have a higher tendency of failure to pay or did they have a high success rate in paying back? The credit scoring model is constantly updated and the weightings given to each component are not revealed for fear of applications being 'tweaked' to improve the chances of getting a 'yes'.

The downside with requesting lower amounts is that the outcome of the credit scoring model has little to do with 'you' – it's the facts presented and that's it. Whilst there is usually an appeal option for the Manager if the answer has come back as a 'no' it can be difficult to get this overturned.

It will be interesting to see how lending assessed via a credit scoring model has held up during the recent recession. Were the assumptions used in building the model robust enough to weed out the poorer performers? Or will we see a return to the days of an individual saying 'yes' instead of hearing 'the computer says no'?

Manager's Personal Lending Limit

I mentioned earlier that Managers may have personal lending limits up to which they can make their own decisions. Over recent years, this has been removed in favour of the next route we will look at but in case you are lucky enough to have a Manager with a personal lending limit then life can be a little easier.

In this situation the Manager will prepare a report for the file outlining all the key areas reviewed, giving his reasons as to why he supports the application or not, as the case may be.

Centralised Review and Approval

If your Manager doesn't have a lending limit, or the amount you have requested is higher than his personal limit, then your request will be referred to a higher authority.

Your Manager will review your request as if he were taking the decision himself, and based on your Business Plan, the interview and all the other information he has gleaned, he will compile a report and then submit to the appropriate department. Because the decision to support you is taken by someone who has never met you, it's vital that your Manager correctly represents you and your business in his report. The person reviewing your request can only base his decision on the information in front of him. You should now see why a Business Plan is so important – this document is written by you, not the Manager, so there will be no mixed or misunderstood messages.

If you have provided all the necessary information and answered all the questions put to you then you can be confident that your Manager will effectively represent you when presenting your case to his boss.

Once the decision has been made, all that remains is for the Manager to tell you the good news or the bad news!

After The Decision Has Been Made

When you finally get that all important phone call giving you the feedback you have waited for there will be one of three outcomes:

- More information is required before a decision can be made
- Your request has been declined
- Your request has been agreed

Let's have a look at each of these possible outcomes and see what you need to do or can expect to happen.

More Information Needed

When you get a request for more information it merely means that the Manager didn't get all the information that was necessary for him to reach a decision. There is a note of optimism hidden here - it means that at least your application has not been totally dismissed! There must be something in your idea or request that he likes, otherwise he would not be wasting his time or yours by asking for more details.

Your Request Has Been Declined

The first thing you need to do is to find out why your application was not successful. You need to get specifics so that:

- You can understand the weaknesses in your Plan
- You can put the weaknesses right and try again, either with the same bank or a different one
- You can decide whether you need to have a complete re-think of your idea
- You can seek other sources of non-bank funding, especially if you get the feedback which basically says, 'Don't waste your time coming back!' We covered these sources earlier in the book.

Ask which part of the application let you down. Once you know the problem, you are in a better position to put it right. This could include you commissioning an independent review of your business to prove viability. We will be looking at Independent Business Reviews later but whilst such reviews are usually at the behest of the bank in response to worrying warning signs, you can call for one if you feel it would help your case for finance.

Don't discount the fact that personality may have come into play here. It's a fact of life that we don't get on with all the people we do business with. If you think the Manager has not 'heard' your proposal don't be afraid to go over his head to challenge the answer and to seek another opinion; do whatever you can to ensure you are given every opportunity to get your case across.

If you are not successful, it's important to be objective about it. Shouting and screaming at the Manager is not going to help your case, especially if you decide to re-submit your request at a later stage! Coming across as a "hot-head" will not improve your reputation.

You can talk to many successful business people and you will find that at some stage in their careers they faced problems with their banks but they battled on. They may tell you that rejection can sometimes be the turning point of success; the bank turning you down may lead to changes being made which are for the better.

Rejection can be a blessing in disguise as long as you take action to learn and adapt. I have dealt with a number of successful business people over the years who have been turned down but they don't let rejection drag them down; if anything it spurs them on! Don't be put off by a "no" answer and be one of those people who fall at the first hurdle and never bother getting up.

Why Your Application Could Have Been Declined

- Your Business Plan was weak and didn't accurately reflect your business and its potential

- You did not convincingly show your ability to repay the amount requested. Did your forecasts need better explanation?

- Has your bank account been poorly run with a history of bounced cheques? Did you acknowledge this problem and show how you are addressing it?

- Has the bank misunderstood an important part of the business or misinterpreted a vital part of the Business Plan?

- Is your business in a sector which the bank is not interested in for policy reasons? Find out if this is temporary or whether you should look elsewhere for support.

If you decide not to appeal the decision one alternative route is to seek out another bank. Whilst you may think the answer will be the same don't forget that banks have differing perceptions of risk. If you can't face walking up and down the High Street knocking on every door then you can approach a Commercial Loan Broker who will hunt out the best deal for you. They will charge for their services but at least you have a better chance of success. You can find your nearest broker by accessing the search facility on the National Association of Commercial Loan Brokers' site:

www.nacfb.org/broker.html

However, having said all this, during the credit crunch stories abound of businesses being declined facilities for no real apparent reason. As we have mentioned before, we have seen a time where illogical decisions are being made. When you are up against this there is little to do except find alternative ways to move forward.

Your Loan Has Been Granted

The third outcome of your request is that the overdraft or loan has been approved. You're on your way! All that hard work has paid off! Once the euphoria has died down, especially if your request was to help you start up, you need to find out the procedure and timing to draw down the new facility.

"So when can I access my cash?"

This is probably the most frequently asked question! Before you can get your hands on the cash, there are a few matters to attend to.

Security

If you are providing additional security or new security you will need to sign all the legal documentation before you can access the funds. Don't expect the bank to trust you to sign the legal documentation *after* you have had the money; there always seems to be more important things for you to do than going to the bank to "sign a lot of paper"! In my experience, once business owners have their money, keeping the Bank Manager happy is not a priority. The bank does not want to spend the next six months chasing you!

Sometimes you can sign the documentation on the bank premises but if you have an unconnected 3rd party supporting your loan with their own assets they may have to go to a solicitor to have the implications explained of what they are doing.

Confirmation Letter

Once your request has been agreed the bank will issue a letter of confirmation, which you will be required to acknowledge. The Offer

Letter, or Facility Letter, outlines the terms and conditions on which the bank is agreeing to lend to you. The purpose of confirming everything in writing is to ensure there are no misunderstandings at a later stage and to act as a legal acknowledgement of the debt once the facilities are drawn.

Financial and Other Covenants

Financial and other restrictive covenants are not usually seen in lending to small and medium sized businesses; they tend to be reserved for much larger and riskier loans. Examples of such covenants though would be:

- To meet certain financial ratios such as a liquidity ratio figure, a minimum Net Worth figure or a maximum gearing ratio
- A restriction on the amount of dividends that can be paid out
- A ceiling on further borrowing
- A constraint on future capital investment to preserve liquidity
- To supply monthly or quarterly Management Accounts

A monitoring system will be put in place to ensure that the covenants are met.

The letter will cover the following areas:

- The name of the person or company being lent to
- The type of facility, whether it be an overdraft or loan, as well as a list of current facilities
- The amount being borrowed
- A description of what the facility is being used for
- The repayment terms. If you are being granted an overdraft then

there won't be a specific repayment programme, unless the facility is being used for a specific purpose and the repayment date can be clearly identified. Usually an overdraft continues from year to year and so a date will be shown for the next facility review.

When borrowing via an overdraft an "on demand" clause is included. This means that at any time the bank can demand its money back. This is the drawback of borrowing via overdraft. If you have a loan, as long as you keep up the repayments the bank cannot take action. If you're taking a loan then the letter will quote the date by which the loan will be repaid and how much the monthly repayment is.

- The interest rate you are being charged split into the current Base Rate and the additional margin
- The Arrangement Fee
- The security being given or details of what is already in place
- Any covenants or financial targets which have to be met
- If you are transferring your account from another bank you will be required to make the move prior to the release of funds

Once you have satisfied everything, all that remains is for you to draw down your overdraft or loan and be successful!

Or is it ...?

KEEPING A BEADY EYE ON YOU

Once you have the cash you need all you want to do is put your head down and get on with making money. However, the bank will still want to keep in regular contact, hassling you for figures and taking up your valuable time!

Why do they insist on all those meetings and reviews and keep requesting financial information from you? By the end of this chapter you will understand the usefulness of all those requests.

Why Regular Reviews Are Important

Handing the money over is not the extent of the Manager's responsibility to you and the bank. It's a fact of life that despite how carefully a Manager assesses a request to borrow money, things do go wrong:

- The sector you are in suddenly faces a crisis
- You lose a major supplier or customer
- A competitor arrives on the scene and knocks your margins for six

All of these events, and others, are outside your control and the bank doesn't want a surprise one day to find out that your business is on its knees and either facing closure, or even more worryingly, already closed.

To keep an eye on the safety of its money, the bank will review your account on a regular basis but at least once a year. The depth of information requested, the questions asked, or the frequency of visits does depend on the bank's perception of its risk. If your business is showing early signs of distress or already in trouble then you can expect more frequent contact, which for you may not be a bad thing.

Throughout these visits the bank is assessing how your business is performing and trying to understand the problems you are facing - forewarned is forearmed! Many business people see these regular chats as a waste of time but they do serve a purpose.

Too often, business owners do not share information with their bankers early enough. If they had they may have discovered that the bank could have helped and, perish the thought, given some advice! If a review is confined to once a year, then a position which has been deteriorating for a few months may go undetected until it's too late.

I have had so many instances where problems have arisen and the bank was the last to know. Even if I had not been able to do anything it would have been good to know. In those instances, my view of the owner's trustworthiness took a big dive. You don't want this to happen so during reviews, and even outside of them, share everything.

There's a saying, "Trust is good but information is better." Your Manager may trust you ...but only so far!

The Tools to Regularly Monitor Your Performance

The Manager has a number of tools in his kitbag to assist in monitoring your business. The four main tools are:

- Visits
- Internal records
- Updates on the value of security
- Management figures

Visits

I have already highlighted the benefits of the bank visiting your business premises. A one-off visit when the bank is assessing your request is not going to help in the on-going monitoring of a business. An annual visit will allow your Manager to keep up to date with what is happening within the business, see if there are any changes, both good and bad, and check that the bank's investment is still safe.

Internal Bank Records

The bank's own records can provide some insight into how the business is doing. We have already seen that one of the main tools the bank has to review the performance of an account is the month-by-month history of best, worst and average balances.

Your Manager will regularly refer to this history as it gives a very good overview of how the business is performing (assuming of course that all business transactions are channelled through the bank account). However, there are likely to be reasons or explanations behind certain trends and so the bank will not rely purely on the figures, they will use it as a basis to ask questions and to understand what is happening.

In addition to this ad hoc check on how your account is performing, many banks have reports produced on a regular basis, usually monthly, which highlight accounts that are beginning to show worrying trends.

Such trends could be:

- Frequent breaches of the agreed overdraft limit
- Average overdrawn balance which is increasing each month
- Cheques being returned unpaid
- Credits paid into the account have been reducing in number and value (this could indicate reducing sales or the possibility that funds are being paid into another bank)

Having reviewed these reports, it may be possible that your Manager knows some of the reasons why your account has been reported; if he doesn't, then he'll call you to attend a meeting so he can understand what has caused the change in trend.

Review of Security Value

Although the bank's primary concern is serviceability of a loan or overdraft, it will also keep an eye on its security just to make sure it maintains the initial valuation figure and that it still exists!

Each type of security is reviewed in a different way.

Land

When land is first pledged as security the bank will have it valued. The purpose of this is twofold: to find out how much it's worth and whether there are potential obstacles that can detract from it being easily sold.

Obviously, the market for property and the condition of the building can change over time, so the bank will want to revalue it on a periodic basis. The usual revaluation period is 3 years but if the business performance is good and the account has operated well, the bank may be persuaded not to request a revaluation, thereby saving you the cost.

Directors' Guarantees

Depending on the performance of the business, the bank may periodically check whether the guarantor is still good for the amount of his guarantee, especially if the guarantor is not directly related to the business, i.e. not a director. So if a colleague has guaranteed your overdraft facility of £50,000, the bank may write to his bankers every few years asking whether he could settle a claim under his guarantee for that amount.

If the initial answer, when the guarantee was taken, had been positive, and then three years later it's less than favourable, the bank may approach the borrower for more security, especially if the guarantee is being heavily relied upon. People's fortunes shift, so regular assessment of the guarantee is important.

Again, if the business is performing well and there are no signs of stress it's likely this security check will be overlooked.

Life Policies

As long as the premiums are being kept up to date the life policy will remain in force and so no checks are needed. When taking a legal charge over a life policy, the bank will have advised the life company that it has an interest in the policy, so if premiums do lapse the company would inform the bank. The bank then has the option of bringing the premiums up to date in order to keep the policy in force, or letting the policy lapse.

If the policy is an endowment type which, in addition to life cover, has a surrender value that builds up each year, the bank may periodically enquire on the value of the policy. This would happen if the eventual maturity payment is the ultimate source of repayment. The last few years have seen policy and Unit Trust values decline in line with the financial markets' performance. Any significant shortfall in valuation may prompt the bank to request additional security to plug the deficit.

Stocks and Shares

As we mentioned earlier shares are not the ideal type of security because their value can fluctuate. In order to ensure that a satisfactory margin is maintained between the amount outstanding on the loan and the share value, the price will be regularly monitored. If the value, and so the margin of security, is declining then the bank may ask for additional security to close the gap.

Management Figures

Depending on the size of your business and level of borrowing, your bank may have made it a condition of lending that you supply regular management figures. As we saw earlier, management figures provide an overview performance on a weekly, monthly or quarterly basis. When supplied to the bank the figures can be used to monitor performance on a timelier basis than waiting for receipt of annual accounts. This means problems can be quickly spotted and corrective action taken.

Management accounts are the primary tool for monitoring compliance with financial covenants agreed as part of the funding package. Even if you are not borrowing you should be producing regular figures in order to keep on top of your performance.

Financial and Other Covenants

If your borrowing is on loan, as long as you keep up the repayments, the bank can't call in your debt. However, there could be circumstances where the bank feels uncomfortable with the safety of its lending, for example because of continued losses or undisclosed borrowing from another bank which has come to light.

To cover these situations, the Facility Letter, as we saw earlier, may contain triggers, or events, which give the bank the opportunity to call in the lending.

To identify when a covenant is breached regular monitoring is undertaken via an agreed reporting format and timescale.

A regular review of both business performance and security is just as important as the very first assessment. Regular reviews can help spot problems earlier and so action can be taken to put the business back on track. Don't see the reviews as a burden and a paper generating exercise; they do have value and play an important role in the banker/business relationship.

However, despite close monitoring, things do go wrong and the key for both the bank and you is to spot problems early enough and take immediate and decisive corrective action. In the next chapter we will be looking at the warning signs and what you can do to halt a slide.

LOAN SHARP

WHAT TO DO IF IT STARTS TO GO WRONG

Unfortunately it's a fact of life that too many businesses close down, jobs are lost, owners' lives ruined and homes put up for sale. Some of these outcomes can be avoided if problems, whether actual or potential, are identified early enough and action taken to put them right.

In this chapter we are going to look at the warning signs and the steps that can be taken to prevent the worst from happening.

Warning Signs

Throughout this book you will have picked up the negative points which can "turn-off" a banker. As well as being reasons not to lend money, these negative points can also be considered as a warning sign, an indication that things are not going well within a business.

The business environment is such that it is always changing, always on the move. Every business has to keep up with that change and keep pace otherwise they become inefficient, uncompetitive and unattractive to customers. This inability to keep up doesn't happen overnight, it's a gradual process. This is where the problem lies, the change is *gradual* – you don't see it happening because the changes are small, nothing of significance to make you sit up and take action.

Knowing what to look out for in advance can help you prevent a crisis occurring in the first place. Let's look at some of the key signs of impending trouble. Review these signals against where your business stands today and consider whether any apply to you. If so, what actions can you take to put them right?

Warning Signs from Financial Statements

- Accounts are late being finalised
- The accountant qualifies the accounts with a statement which is effectively a 'health warning'
- An unusually high audit fee
- Frequent change in auditors
- Two sets of accounts – one actual, one for the taxman!
- Assets frequently re-valued
- Reducing Net Worth
- Directors' loans withdrawn or reducing
- Too much short term debt and not enough long term debt
- High gearing
- Deteriorating liquidity
- Slippage in debtor collection period
- Extended credit taken from suppliers
- Stock taking longer to shift
- Sales increasing at a rate less than inflation
- Gross profit margin falling
- Overheads compared to sales are increasing
- Net profit margin falling
- Interest cover reducing

Warning Signs from Management Figures

- Same warning signs as with Financial Statements
- Figures not detailed enough
- Full year's management figures differ significantly from the final annual accounts
- Stock figure shown in round amounts
- Financial covenants not met
- Liquid surplus reducing or deficit increasing
- Creditors increasing or not being met
- Profit and Loss or Cash Flow Forecast not being achieved

Warning Signs from Premises and Management

- Premises don't create a good impression
- Everything is in a poor state of repair which signals ongoing under-investment
- No "buzz" or feeling of activity
- Evidence of dead or long unsold stock
- Top of the range or premium brand vehicles for directors
- Hard to arrange an appointment with owners or directors
- Promises or deadlines for submission of information not being met
- Lack of forward planning
- No understanding of the wider market or competition
- Young management team with little experience
- Old management team who are out of touch
- Poor mix of management talent
- No management succession plan

- Constant change of personnel in the key positions
- Excessive remuneration or expenses
- No understanding of financial performance
- Small customer base
- Evidence of attempting to raise finance elsewhere
- Adverse publicity in local press

Warning Signs from Bank Statements

- Regular breach of the overdraft limit, or going overdrawn with no limit agreed
- Increasing use of the overdraft limit on month-by-month basis
- Deteriorating balances – overdraft going up; credit balances reducing
- Reducing credit turnover
- Cheques being returned unpaid
- Cheques being issued in round amounts
- Cheques regularly being stopped to prevent cheques being returned unpaid
- Large amounts of cash being paid in and withdrawn almost simultaneously

These warning signs in isolation may not be of concern but two or three or more should be a red flag to all parties.

The key to avoiding problems is spotting the signs early enough. You can become blind to the obvious signs that things are not going right. Whilst the bank will be in the background keeping an eye on you they will serve no purpose if you are not prepared to listen to the messages coming your way. In response to a question which is too close to home can you hear yourself saying, "It's only a blip" or

"Things will get better" and you carry on in exactly the same way? Before you know it, it's all over, then the "If only I'd ..." statements start.

Don't disregard the people who are more likely to see the problems you choose to ignore.

The Cycle of Decline

Once a business starts to decline problems multiply and the descent can be like a runaway train, it just goes faster and faster until there comes a point where nothing can prevent an almighty crash.

To help you spot the danger signals here is a typical cycle of decline:

- Sales start to decline but no proactive steps are taken to halt the decline or curb overheads
- The distraction caused by a fall in business means that debtor collection slips and cash collection slows
- Pressure builds up on the bank account with the overdraft limit being breached more regularly
- As cash becomes tight payments to creditors are postponed
- The overdraft limit is breached once too often without prior agreement by the bank
- Cheques are returned unpaid by the bank
- Creditors start getting nervous and refuse to extend further credit
- Creditors reduce existing credit terms causing a further squeeze on cash
- In an effort to get more cash in, stock is reduced, buying of new stock curtailed and the debtor collection process is finally reviewed; debtors are chased to pay up; discounts on invoices

are offered in exchange for early payment

- Management's attention gets diverted to dealing with the impending cash crisis and the pursuit of new business, and taking care of existing customers and product quality disappears from day-to-day activity

- Because they are being pressurised to pay up customers sense that something is wrong and begin to look elsewhere for alternative suppliers in order to spread their risk

- With stock purchases reduced, turnaround times slow down and sales slip as more customers go elsewhere

- With sales reducing cash gets even tighter and it becomes increasingly difficult to deal with all the creditors; the bank becomes even more nervous

- Eventually there is no more stock to sell; all the "good" debts have been collected leaving only the ones who can't or won't pay; sales have fallen; creditors are pushing for payment and the end is in sight

Whilst some of these points in isolation are good for the business in that they may release extra cash into the system you see how the cycle starts and once the momentum is in full flow the decline has a life of its own.

This scenario can be prevented if both the bank and the business owner act soon enough in response to the warning signs. This is the key - early action. Too often business owners will ignore the signs and bury their heads in the sand, hoping the problems will be rectified in time with no intervention - it usually doesn't happen this way.

If the bank is requesting regular figures from you and making frequent visits then they should have spotted the problem trends early enough and so prompted you to take action. However, if you are a relatively small business, it's possible that the bank will not have been asking for regular figures or talking to you and so you are on your own. It's then down to you to realise there is a problem and to take corrective action.

Actions You Can Take

Knowing there's something wrong and not doing anything about it is just as bad as not knowing at all.

Here are some actions you can take.

Speak to the Bank

The first thing you should do is speak to your Manager. Most business owners think this is the last thing you should do! They think the bank will panic and close them down! Wrong. It's not in the bank's interest to take that sort of action so early in the cycle. Caught early enough, the bank can help solve the problem and give advice on the actions to take. Of course, this is what you would expect during a 'normal' business cycle! I'm sure you have all heard stories of where a bank has moved too quickly to the detriment of the business. As I have said previously, we are not in 'normal' times; sense will return so it's important that the basic premise of communication is not forgotten.

Talking to your Manager can help; it will bring a different perspective, a new set of eyes and possible solutions. Too many business owners try and exclude the bank from the problems they are having, when they should actually be bringing the bank in. Hiding things from your Manager has a number of consequences:

- When he finds out that you have known about a problem for some time, an element of mistrust builds up. Once lost, trust is hard to rebuild and it is during difficult times that you need his trust and support.

- A solution may have been possible if the problem had been raised sooner. If the bank is told later on, the problem may be too far gone for them to help.

Being up front and keeping in touch is essential if you are to ride out any problems.

See Your Accountant

Accountants see problematic situations all the time and, just as with a chat with the Bank Manager, your accountant will be able to provide help and guidance. He may be able to help you put together a revised Business Plan which can then be taken to the bank to show you have a grip on the problem and that you are taking the necessary steps to put things right.

Your accountant can also review your financial reporting systems and make appropriate suggestions if they see this as one of the causes of your problems. Accountants today are much more than 'number crunchers'. If you pick the right one they can bring a new perspective to your business in the way of systems, controls and checks.

Business Colleagues

You may be unwilling to share your problems with fellow entrepreneurs but they can be a good source of advice. Pick the one who has "been there, done that" or one who can point you in the direction of someone who has. Make sure you pick the right person – someone you can trust, whose opinion you will value and with whom there will be no conflict of interest.

Talking through business problems can save you re-inventing the wheel as very few problems are totally unique to you. Sharing your problems is not a sign of weakness.

Enterprise Agencies

These government funded agencies give free and impartial advice. The trained advisors, just like your Bank Manager and accountant, may be able to come up with creative solutions to your problems to get you back on track.

Some people have had mixed experiences with such advisors so ask around and see if you can get the name of someone with a good reputation.

Independent Assessments

Depending on the size of your business and borrowings, if the warning signs are of sufficient concern, the bank may insist on an independent business assessment.

Carried out by independent accountants, or licensed insolvency practitioners, their brief is to review your operation to identify where the business stands now, and what can be done to improve performance and re-establish long-term viability.

Such a review is only done for businesses that have a good chance of continuing to trade and where the directors have shown willingness to listen and implement any plan of action detailed in the final report.

What Does The Review Cover?

There is an agreed programme to follow to ensure that as much as possible is achieved by the review. The review will assess the following areas:

- The existing management structure
- Current financial position
- Review of Financial Statements and management figures (if available)

- Review of budgets and cash flow forecasts
- Suggested areas for profit improvement
- Comments on the bank's security position
- Assessment of long term viability
- Agreed action plan

The reviewer will have a series of meetings with key members of the management team to understand the business and the issues they are facing. During this process, in order to get the most from the review, it's advisable to be as open and honest as possible. This is your chance to identify your problem areas and to get the business back on its feet, so seize the opportunity.

Following the Advice

When the report has been finalised there are four likely options for both the bank and business to consider:

- The business should cease trading immediately and the assets sold to repay liabilities. In this instance there is no hope of salvaging the business. If the directors of the business refuse to cooperate then the bank may look at the various Corporate Insolvency options available to it in order to safeguard its position.

- The business should be put on the market and sold as a going concern, which will attract a higher price than a business being closed and sold piecemeal. This may involve the bank providing additional financial support pending a sale.

- The business is basically sound and support should be continued at the same level, with no further borrowing, but subject to some internal changes and other recommendations being acted upon.

- The same position as in the previous point but with the recommendation that further funds are advanced to keep the business going until the suggested actions are implemented.

Future Monitoring

If the review report confirms that the business has a long term future then, as long as the agreed actions are followed, the bank will probably continue its support.

Once the decision to carry on has been made the bank may insist that the reviewer undertakes a regular follow-up to ensure that everything is going to plan. This may take the form of a brief monthly report or an in-depth quarterly or six-monthly review. The monitoring report would include comments on:

- Trading performance
- General financial position
- Performance against any revised forecasts
- Review of the action plan to see that the agreed actions are being implemented
- If necessary, an update of the bank's security position
- Any revisions to the action plan which are needed to keep the business on track

The Cost

The business owner's main bone of contention is usually the cost. It's not free and it's usually not cheap. However, if you are faced with this situation you have to accept that your business is at a crossroads; not accepting the review could lead to an uncertain future.

If you are in any doubt as to whether it will be worthwhile, ask your bank if they can introduce you to a business which has gone through the process. The bank will obviously have to obtain agreement from the other party before releasing their name to you and if they accept, you should take the opportunity to ask what benefits they had from the review.

One point to emphasise though is that you may not have any choice in agreeing to the review. If the bank is uncomfortable in extending further facilities the only way they will feel happy is by having an independent assessment. If this is what it takes to secure a future for your business, then you just have to accept it.

Your other option, of course, is to seek new bankers who are prepared to grant you the facilities you need but that can take time - anything up to four to six weeks from start to finish (or if you speak to some business owners, even longer). However, if there are clear warning signs that your business is struggling, the chances of moving banks may be very slim.

Agree a Course of Action

After having reviewed all the possible actions you can take, go back to the bank and formally set out what action you are taking.

Your plan may include reducing staff numbers, cutting back on specific overheads, dropping an unprofitable product, or agreeing to the independent review. Don't go into denial – "I don't really have to do this – another way will come up soon." If you have come to the realisation that your business is in trouble then it's likely the bank will have as well. You cannot take the risk of the bank taking the lead and starting legal action against you or the business. They *will* do this if you stop talking to them or dig your heels in. Accept what has to be done and cooperate.

Working with the bank, instead of against it, will go a long way in respect of a future relationship. Remember, your track record is important.

Being in a situation such as this is difficult to accept but many small business owners have faced this crossroads and have come out of it on the other side with a leaner and more efficient business.

Tackle the problems, take the necessary decisions and move on.

CONCLUSION

Here we are at the end of the book, but at the start of your journey.

I have shown you the way to get inside the Bank Manager's mind. By now you will have a clear understanding of what you need to do to get him on your side. If you have an established track record and a history of profitable trading then you will find access to finance easier but it may take longer than you were previously used to. For start ups or existing businesses with ambitious growth plans then the going will be tougher. You may not get it right first time but with this book, and the learning points you will get from each meeting with the bank, you will be on your way to securing the finance you need.

There are two final messages I want to leave with you with:

- Preparation is vital. Now you know what's needed, even if you don't require money today, start your preparation. Get your Financial Statements up to date; start preparing monthly management accounts; play around with preparing Cash Flow Forecasts so you can get used to the process; learn your numbers and calculate your ratios; and start writing your Business Plan

- Communication is the key to a successful relationship with the bank. Understand how they operate, what they want and how they want it. Understand the importance of talking to the bank regularly; treat them as a partner in your business, because in reality that is what they are.

The last few years have been tough for a cordial business/banker relationship and many of the points I have covered may not resonate with you as regards your recent experiences. Yes, the rules of the game have changed, probably for good as bad memories tend to last many years, and so you have your part to play in getting your relationship back on track. Follow the ideas and tips we have covered and you will be well on your way to creating a successful and profitable relationship.

I would be delighted to hear from you so please check out the Business Loan Services website (www.businessloanservices.co.uk) for contact details and more information on getting the best out of your bank.

Lightning Source UK Ltd.
Milton Keynes UK

176099UK00001B/27/P